I0438887

Disclaimer

Book Title: 1994 Northridge Earthquake: Performance of Structures, Lifelines and Fire Protection Systems (NIST SP 862)

Book Author: Nicholas J. Carino; R M. Chung; Hai S. Lew; A W. Taylor; William D. Walton;

Book Abstract: A magnitude 6.8 (Ms) earthquake centered under the community of Northridge in the San Fernando Valley shook the entire Los Angeles metropolitan area at 4:31 a.m. local time on Monday, January 17, 1994. Moderate damage to the built environment was widespread; severe damage included collapsed buildings and highway overpasses. A total of 58 deaths were attributed to the earthquake by the Los Angeles Coroner. About 1,500 people were admitted to hospitals with major injuries; another 16,000 or so were treated and released. Estimates of the number of people temporarily or permanently displaced because of damage to their houses or apartments ranged from 80,000 to 125,000. Estimates indicate that this will be the United States' most costly natural disaster ever. A multi-agency team, organized under the auspices of the Interagency Committee on Seismic Safety in Construction and headed by the National Institute of Standards and Technology, arrived at the earthquake site within days of the event to document the effects of the earthquake. The team focused on the effects to the built environment, with the goal of capturing perishable data and quickly identifying situations deserving in-depth study. This report includes a summary of the team's observations. While most structural damage occurred in buildings and bridges of construction type and vintage known to be vulnerable to earthquake shaking, there were some unexpected failures. Notable among these were the collapses of relatively modern parking structures and a bridge that appeared to be adequate by today's standards. Recommendations are made for further studies of the Northridge earthquake that can lead to improved mitigation of earthquake effects. SEE ALSO: NISTIR 5396

Citation: NIST SP - 862

Keyword: earthquakes; bridges (structures); building technology; building fires; lifelines; overpasses; seismic

NIST Special Publication 862

(ICSSC TR14)

1994 Northridge Earthquake
Performance of Structures, Lifelines, and Fire Protection Systems

Diana Todd
Nicholas Carino
Riley M. Chung
H. S. Lew
Andrew W. Taylor
William D. Walton
James D. Cooper
Roland Nimis

Building and Fire Research Laboratory
National Institute of Standards and Technology
Gaithersburg, MD 20899-0001

Federal Highway Administration
Department of Transportation
Washington, DC

May 1994

U.S. Department of Commerce
Ronald H. Brown, Secretary

Technology Administration
Mary L. Good, Under Secretary for Technology

National Institute of Standards and Technology
Arati Prabhakar, Director

ABSTRACT

A magnitude 6.8 (M_s) earthquake centered under the community of Northridge in the San Fernando Valley shook the entire Los Angeles metropolitan area at 4:31 a.m. local time on Monday, January 17, 1994. Moderate damage to the built environment was widespread; severe damage included collapsed buildings and highway overpasses. A total of 58 deaths were attributed to the earthquake by the Los Angeles Coroner. About 1,500 people were admitted to hospitals with major injuries; another 16,000 or so were treated and released. Estimates of the number of people temporarily or permanently displaced because of damage to their houses or apartments ranged from 80,000 to 125,000. Estimates indicate that this will be the United States' most costly natural disaster ever.

A multi-agency team, organized under the auspices of the Interagency Committee on Seismic Safety in Construction and headed by the National Institute of Standards and Technology, arrived at the earthquake site within days of the event to document the effects of the earthquake. The team focused on the effects to the built environment, with the goal of capturing perishable data and quickly identifying situations deserving in-depth study. This report includes a summary of the team's observations. While most structural damage occurred in buildings and bridges of construction type and vintage known to be vulnerable to earthquake shaking, there were some unexpected failures. Notable among these were the collapses of relatively modern parking structures and a bridge that appeared to be adequate by today's standards. Recommendations are made for further studies of the Northridge earthquake that can lead to improved mitigation of earthquake effects.

Key words: bridges; building technology; buildings; earthquake; fire; lifelines; Northridge; overpasses; seismic.

TABLE OF CONTENTS

CHAPTER 1

INTRODUCTION

A strong earthquake centered under the community of Northridge in the San Fernando Valley shook the entire Los Angeles area at 4:31 a.m. local time on Monday, January 17, 1994. The surface wave magnitude, originally estimated at 6.6, was later revised upward to 6.8. January 17 was a federal holiday (Martin Luther King's Birthday) and, because of this and the early morning hour, most nonresidential buildings were empty and traffic was light. This fortuitous circumstance helped limit the number of deaths and injuries.

This earthquake, though not as large as the 1989 magnitude 7.1 Loma Prieta earthquake, affected more people and caused more damage because it occurred in a heavily populated area. The epicenter of the Loma Prieta quake was about 95 km from downtown San Francisco, in a sparsely populated region of the Santa Cruz mountains. The epicenter of the Northridge quake was directly beneath a suburban area of houses, apartment buildings, shopping malls, hospitals, schools, and a university campus. Estimates indicate that this will be the United States' most costly natural disaster ever.

1.1 Immediate Impact of the Earthquake

The impact on the built environment was high. Many two and three-story apartment buildings collapsed or were severely damaged. Hundreds of single-family homes suffered minor, but disruptive damage. Several large commercial buildings collapsed. Hundreds of shops and offices were closed because of nonstructural damage such as fallen ceiling tiles and broken glass. Several hospitals were forced to evacuate their patients. The entire Los Angeles County school system was shut down to allow for cleanup and damage repair. Eight large public parking garages suffered partial or complete collapse. Seven major highway bridges were severely damaged or destroyed by the shaking. Water mains broke and flooded streets; gas lines broke and in some instances started significant fires. The entire Los Angeles area lost electric power.

As of Feb. 14, the Los Angeles Department of the Coroner had attributed a total of 58 deaths to the earthquake. About 1500 people were admitted to hospitals with major injuries; another 16 000 or so were treated and released. Estimates of the number of people temporarily or permanently displaced because of damage to their houses or apartments ranged from 80 000 to 125 000. As of early February, over 400 000 people had registered for various types of Federal disaster assistance.

The normal functioning of the Los Angeles area was significantly disrupted by the highway overpass failures. Most people in the area depend on personal automobiles for transportation; the public transportation capacity is not as sizable as in large cities elsewhere in the country.

The failures in the interconnected electric power grid had a wide impact. Power was disrupted briefly throughout the western United States and Canada. Water service was also disrupted. Where water was flowing, a "boil-water" order was in effect in the epicentral region until late January.

Although the earthquake caused unprecedented damage and disruption, it also created an unprecedented opportunity to learn about earthquake mechanisms and effects. The earthquake triggered more recordings of strong-ground motion than have ever been captured before. This information on the response of the ground surface, buildings, and bridges, coupled with wide-reaching damage surveys and analysis of specific structures, can provide a wealth of new insight into and understanding of earthquakes and their effects. Studies of the effectiveness of emergency response and recovery can provide similar new knowledge that can help other communities plan for disasters.

Twenty-three years prior to the Northridge earthquake, the same area was badly shaken by the Richter magnitude 6.6 San Fernando earthquake. The 1971 earthquake was centered about 25 km northeast of the 1994 event. This provides an opportunity for studies to be made comparing the performance of structures, the effectiveness of emergency response, and the robustness of the recovery.

1.2 Overview of Report

Within hours of the quake, The Interagency Committee on Seismic Safety in Construction, a part of the National Earthquake Hazards Reduction Program, began to organize a multi-agency Federal reconnaissance team. Team members included:

National Institute of Standards and Technology
       H.S. Lew
       Riley M. Chung
       Nicholas Carino
       Andrew W. Taylor
       Diana Todd
       William D. Walton
Federal Emergency Management Agency
       Michael Mahoney
Federal Highway Administration
       James Cooper
Department of Housing and Urban Development
       Sam Hacopian
U.S. Geological Survey
       E.V. Leyendecker

Joining the team in the field was Los Angeles resident LeVal Lund, Civil Engineer. Most of the team members arrived in the Northridge area on Wednesday, January 19, 1994. The team noted and documented the effects of the earthquake, focusing on the effects to the built environment and on the performance of lifelines and fire protection systems, with the goal of capturing perishable data and quickly identifying situations deserving in-depth study. The team was also available as a resource to Federal agencies that needed assistance in documenting damage to their facilities.

Chapter 2 of this report presents basic information on seismological aspects of the quake and availability of strong-motion records. Geotechnical effects, such as landslides, liquefaction, and surface rupture, are also reviewed in Chapter 2. In Chapters 3, 4, and 5 the performance of selected buildings, bridges, and lifeline structures, respectively, is discussed. The cause of, spread, and response to earthquake-induced fires are examined in Chapter 6. This report is not a comprehensive compilation of damage. Selected examples of poor and good performance are discussed. The report concludes with recommendations for further studies which can lead to improved earthquake mitigation practices.

CHAPTER 2

SEISMOLOGICAL AND GEOTECHNICAL ASPECTS

2.1 Seismological Aspects

The epicenter of the earthquake that occurred in the Los Angeles area at 4:31 a.m. local time on January 17, 1994, was located at 34°12'N, 118°32'W, about 30 km west-northwest of Los Angeles in Northridge (fig. 2.1). The National Earthquake Information Center has calculated the surface wave magnitude of the quake as $M_s=6.8$, an increase over their original estimate of $M_s=6.6$. The focal depth has been estimated at about 15-20 km [1,2]. The strong shaking lasted about 15 seconds in the epicentral area.

The Northridge earthquake is the largest event to have occurred in the Los Angeles area in this century. The second largest, the Richter magnitude 6.6 San Fernando earthquake of 1971 (also known as the Sylmar earthquake), was centered about 25 km to the northeast of the 1994 epicenter (fig. 2.2). Other notable earthquakes in the area, as documented in *Catalog of Significant Earthquakes 2150 B.C - 1991 A.D*, published by the National Geophysical Data Center [3], include the 1925 magnitude 6.2 Santa Barbara earthquake, the 1933 magnitude 6.4 Long Beach earthquake, the 1973 magnitude 5.9 Oxnard earthquake, the 1987 magnitude 5.9 Whittier Narrows earthquake, and the 1991 magnitude 5.8 Sierra Madre earthquake. In the nineteenth century, a moderate quake with estimated maximum Modified Mercalli Intensity VIII shook the Los Angeles area in 1855 and generated a tsunami. In 1812, forty people were killed by an earthquake at San Juan Capistrano.

The San Andreas fault, generally acknowledged to be the boundary between the North American and Pacific tectonic plates, which in this area trends southeast-northwest about 60 km northeast of Los Angeles, has not experienced a significant earthquake along this portion of its length in the last two centuries. The scenario earthquake dubbed "The Big One" in the media is postulated as a magnitude 8 event occurring on the San Andreas fault.

The Northridge earthquake occurred on an unidentified fault. Because there was no distinct surface rupture, definitive attribution to a specific fault may not be possible. However, records from the mainshock and the aftershocks indicate that the rupture had a thrust focal mechanism, striking 10° north of west and dipping 30° to 45° south [2,4,5] (fig. 2.3). Nearby known faults include the Frew fault and the Santa Susana fault.

The entire San Fernando Valley and adjoining regions such as west and central Los Angeles, Santa Monica, Malibu, Santa Clarita and the Simi Valley, were strongly or moderately shaken. The shaking was reportedly felt as far south as the Mexican border and as far north as Oregon (Los Angeles Times, January 18, 1994). Damage was concentrated in Los Angeles, Orange and Ventura counties.

The aftershock activity is distributed largely to the north and northwest of the mainshock location (fig. 2.2). The Southern California Seismographic Network reports that some aftershocks occurred on the rupture surface of the 1971 event [4]. On the day of the event, two aftershocks greater than magnitude 5 were recorded (5.9 and 5.6). As of late March, 1994, the largest aftershock to have occurred since the date of the main event was a magnitude 5.3 shock on Sunday, March 20, about 9 km east of the epicenter. The March 20 shock was the seventh aftershock of magnitude 5 or greater.

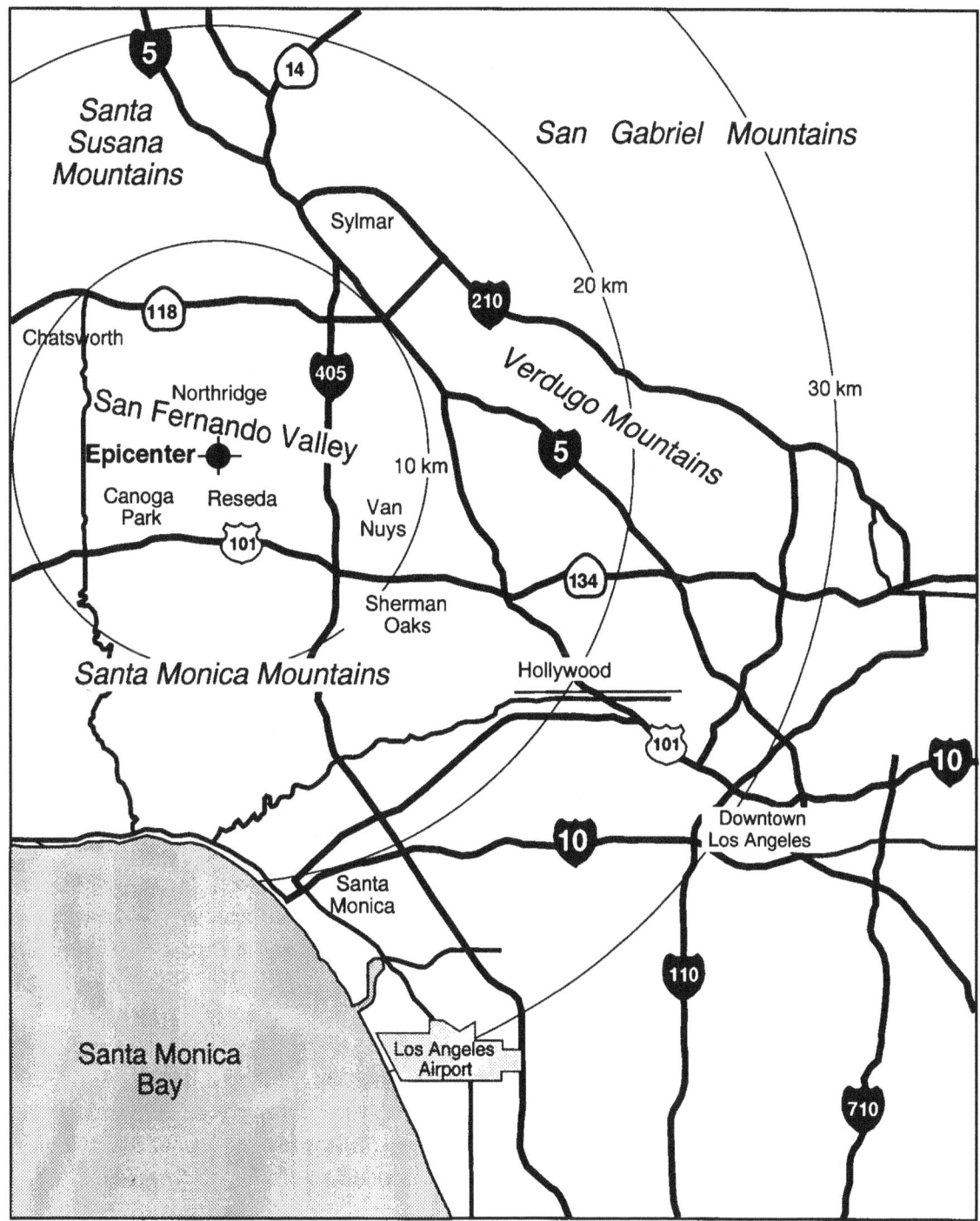

Figure 2.1. The epicenter of the January 17, 1994 Northridge earthquake was centered about 30 km northwest of Los Angeles in the San Fernando Valley.

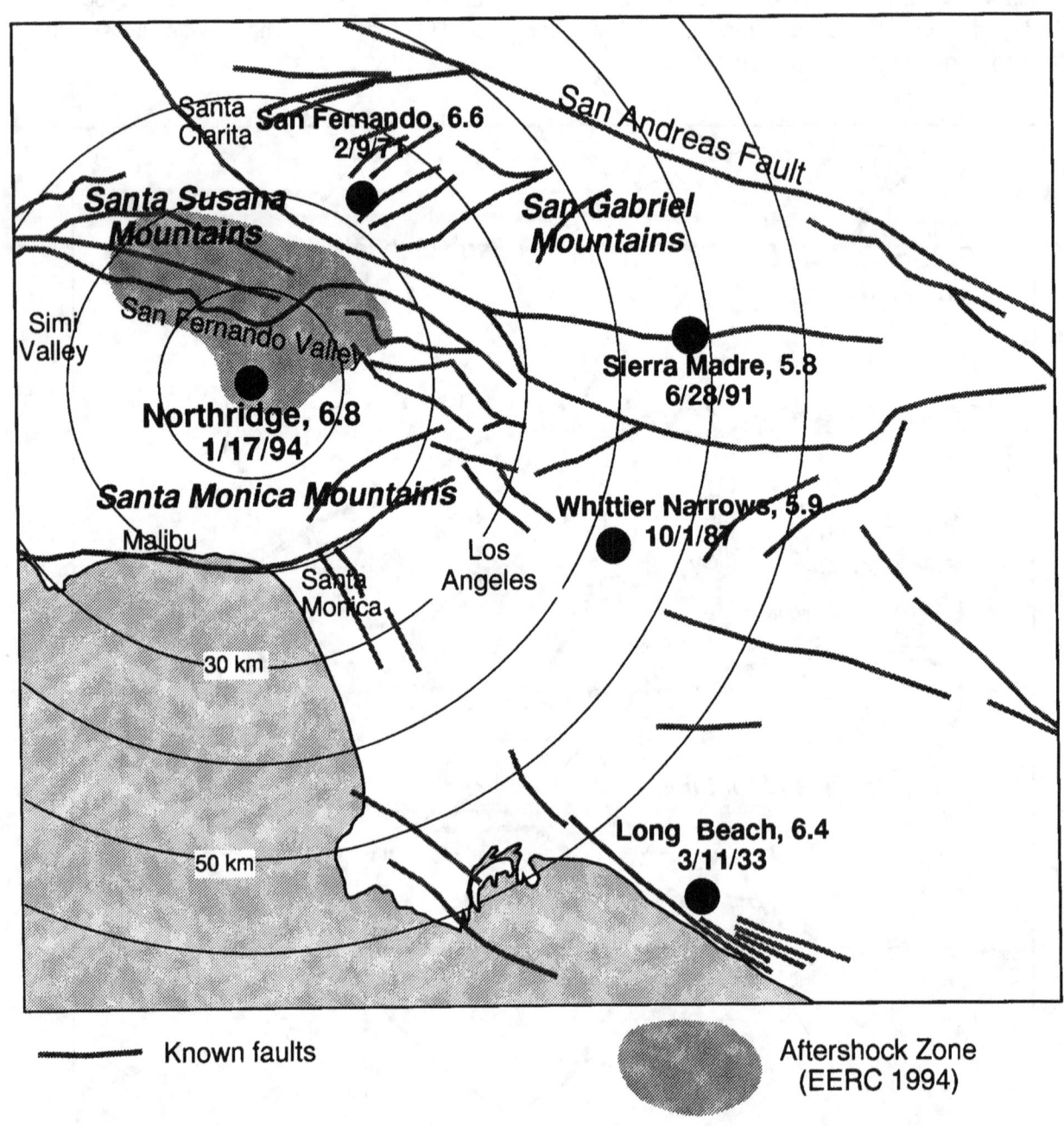

Figure 2.2. The Northridge epicenter was about 25 km southwest of the epicenter of the 1971 magnitude 6.6 San Fernando earthquake. Aftershock activity of the 1994 event has been concentrated to the north and northwest of the epicenter. Other past earthquakes in this area are shown.

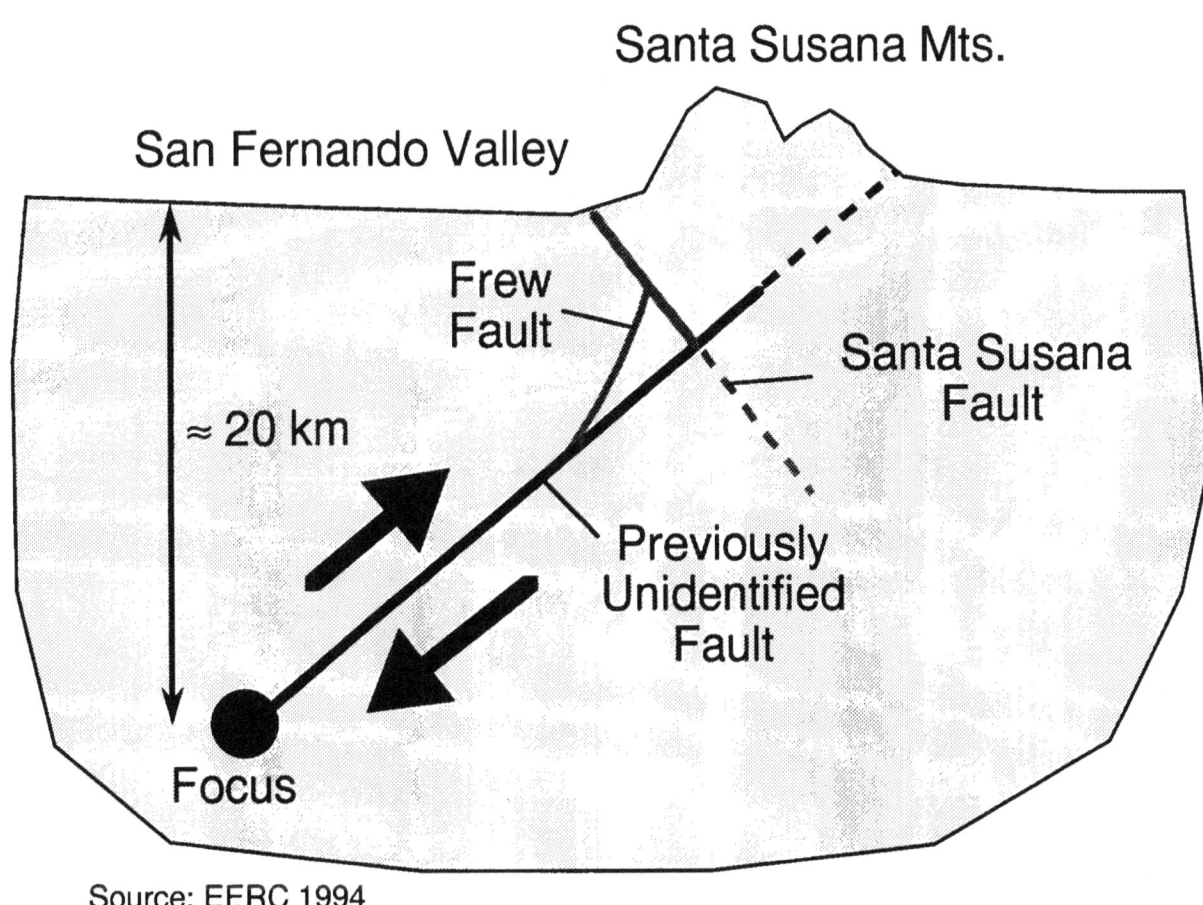

Source: EERC 1994

Figure 2.3.   The mainshock occurred on a previously unidentified thrust fault, near the Frew and Santa Susana faults.

2.2 Strong-Ground Motions

Over a hundred strong-motion recorders were triggered by the event, including instruments operated by the U.S. Geological Survey, the State of California, and several universities. Instruments recorded free-field surface motions as well as the responses of a variety of buildings, bridges, dams, and other structures. Record peak accelerations were recorded, both horizontally and vertically. In the epicentral area, peak horizontal ground accelerations approached or exceeded 1g in several locations [1]. Among the nearly 100 permanent stations operated by the U.S. Geological Survey (USGS), peak horizontal ground accelerations exceeding 0.25g were recorded at 11 sites. The Los Angeles Building Code specifies a design acceleration of 0.4g. Figure 2.4 shows the locations of selected peak horizontal and vertical ground accelerations recorded at sites operated by the USGS's National Strong Motion Program. Table 2.1 lists peak horizontal and vertical accelerations at selected ground and building sites 5 to 38 km from the epicenter. The furthest USGS station triggered was at Skinner Dam, 153 km from the epicenter.

An accelerograph recorded on the grounds of the Veterans Affairs Hospital in Sepulveda is shown in Figure 2.5. Peak horizontal accelerations of 0.74g in the east-west direction and 0.94g in the north-south direction were recorded. These transient peak accelerations were each one-time events and not typical of the body of the shaking. The peak vertical acceleration was 0.48g.

The strong-motion records, when analyzed, will provide a substantial body of information. Preliminary acceleration response spectra show that in some locations and for some periods of motion, the single-degree-of-freedom elastic response (5% damping) induced by the recorded ground accelerations was significantly larger than the spectral acceleration specified as the basis for design by the *Uniform Building Code* [6] for this region.

Figures 2.6 and 2.7, calculated by Hart Consultant Group from strong-motion data from the California Strong Motion Instrumentation Program, present the spectral accelerations for five percent damping of north-south, east-west, and vertical components of motion at two ground sites, in Sylmar and Santa Monica. Also plotted is the lateral seismic design spectrum for the Los Angeles area calculated using the design criteria of the *Uniform Building Code* [6].

In the parking lot of the county hospital in Sylmar, at a distance of about 15 km from the epicenter, spectral accelerations in the north-south direction exceeded the design spectrum across the entire range of periods (fig. 2.6). A significant peak of about 2.5 times the design value occurs between periods of about 0.3 to 0.5 seconds. For periods over 1.2 seconds, values of about two times the design value were calculated. This suggest that both mid-rise and high-rise buildings were severely tested at this location. The spectral accelerations associated with east-west motion exceed the design values for periods from about 0.5 to 1.0 seconds, but not to the extent exhibited by the north-south motion. The peak horizontal acceleration recorded at this site was 0.91g.

On the grounds of the Santa Monica City Hall (fig. 2.7), about 25 km south of the epicenter, it was the east-west component of motion that created significantly high spectral accelerations, exceeding design values by a factor of 1.5 to over 2.5 for periods from 0.1 to 0.5 seconds. Values were at or below the design spectrum for higher periods, indicating that low-rise

9

buildings experienced more violent shaking than mid and high-rise buildings. The north-south component generally did not generate values in excess of the design spectrum at this site. The maximum horizontal acceleration recorded was 0.93g.

These spectral analyses are for two of the most extreme records recovered from this earthquake. When all of the available records have been analyzed, substantial information will be available for a fuller assessment of the appropriateness of the current design spectrum.

The high vertical accelerations recorded in numerous locations have induced discussions among the engineering community over the need to consider vertical accelerations in design. Currently, the model codes that serve as a basis for most building codes in this country only require consideration of vertical accelerations in the design of cantilevered elements and post-tensioned horizontal elements, and those only in regions of high seismicity. In the Northridge event, a free-field vertical acceleration of 1.18g was recorded at Tarzana, about 6 km south of the epicenter, and maximums of about 0.6g occurred at several other locations.

The strong-motion records obtained from instrumented buildings, bridges, and other structures will provide information that can be used to calibrate and improve design and analysis procedures. Some exceptionally high peak response accelerations in structures were recorded: 2.31g horizontal acceleration on the roof of the county hospital in Sylmar; greater than 1.7g vertical on the Pacoima Dam.

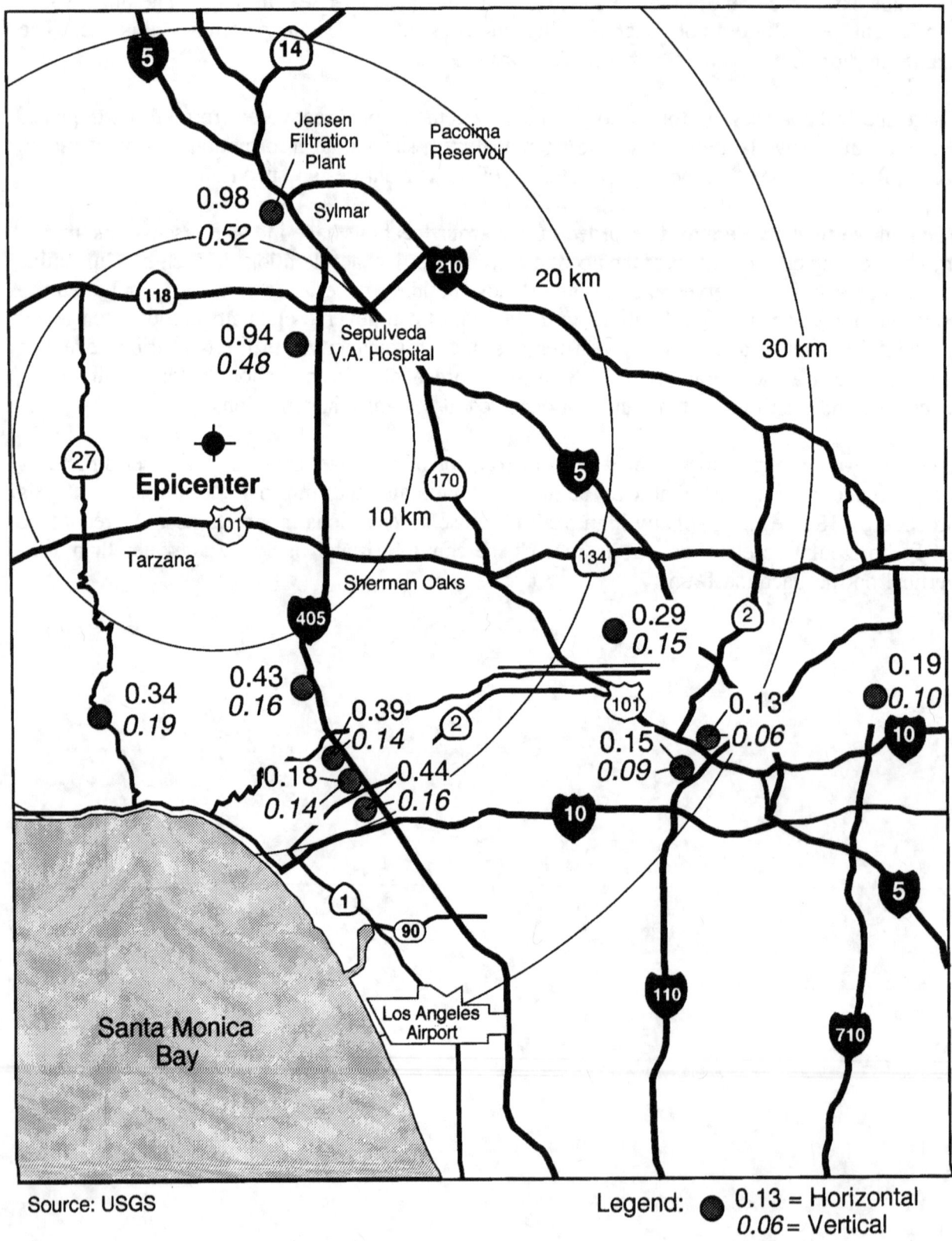

Figure 2.4. Peak horizontal and vertical ground accelerations recorded at some of the instruments in the affected area operated by the USGS's National Strong Motion Program.

Table 2.1. Peak Accelerations, January 17, 1994 Northridge Earthquake.

Location	Epicentral Distance	Peak Accel. Horiz.	Vert.
Los Angeles, 6301 Owensmouth Ave., Roof, 12 stories	5 km	0.48g	0.48g
Los Angeles, Sepulveda VA Hospital, Ground	7 km	0.94g	0.48g
Los Angeles, 5805 Sepulveda Blvd., Roof - 9 stories	7 km	0.76g	0.50g
Los Angeles, 16000 Ventura Blvd., Roof - 13 stories	8 km	0.41g	0.37g
Los Angeles, 15250 Ventura Blvd., Roof - 13 stories	8 km	0.61g	0.43g
Jensen Filter Plant, Administration Building, Basement	12 km	0.62g	0.40g
Jensen Filter Plant, Generator Building, Ground	12 km	0.98g	0.52g
Sepulveda Canyon, Spillway Building, Ground	14 km	0.43g	0.16g
Topanga, Fire Station, Ground	15 km	0.34g	0.19g
Los Angeles, Brentwood VA Hospital, Ground	18 km	0.29g	0.16g
Los Angeles, 10920 Wilshire Blvd., 19th Level	19 km	0.17g	0.24g
Los Angeles, 10751 Wilshire Blvd., Roof - 12 stories	19 km	0.40g	0.39g
Los Angeles, 10660 Wilshire Blvd., Roof - 19 stories	19 km	1.00g	0.51g
Los Angeles, Wadsworth VA Hosp., North Ground Site	19 km	0.26g	0.17g
Los Angeles, Wadsworth VA Hosp., South Ground Site	19 km	0.39g	0.14g
Los Angeles, 2029 Century Park East, 43rd Floor	20 km	0.32g	0.46g
Malibu Canyon, Monte Nido Fire Station, Ground	21 km	0.20g	0.17g
Los Angeles, 2121 Ave. of the Stars, Roof, 36 stories	21 km	0.43g	0.63g
Los Angeles, 1955 1/2 Purdue Ave., Basement	21 km	0.44g	0.16g
Los Angeles, 1955 1/2 Purdue Ave., First Level	21 km	0.50g	0.48g
Los Angeles, 1955 1/2 Purdue Ave., Third Level	21 km	0.63g	0.46g
Los Angeles, Griffith Observatory, Ground	24 km	0.29g	0.15g
Los Angeles, 1111 Sunset Blvd., Basement	31 km	0.13g	0.06g
Los Angeles, 1111 Sunset Blvd., 4th Floor	31 km	0.18g	0.09g
Los Angeles, 1111 Sunset Blvd., Roof - 8 stories	31 km	0.23g	0.16g
Lawndale, 15000 Aviation Blvd., Ground	38 km	0.18g	0.09g

Source: Porcella et al. 1994, USGS Open File Report 94-141

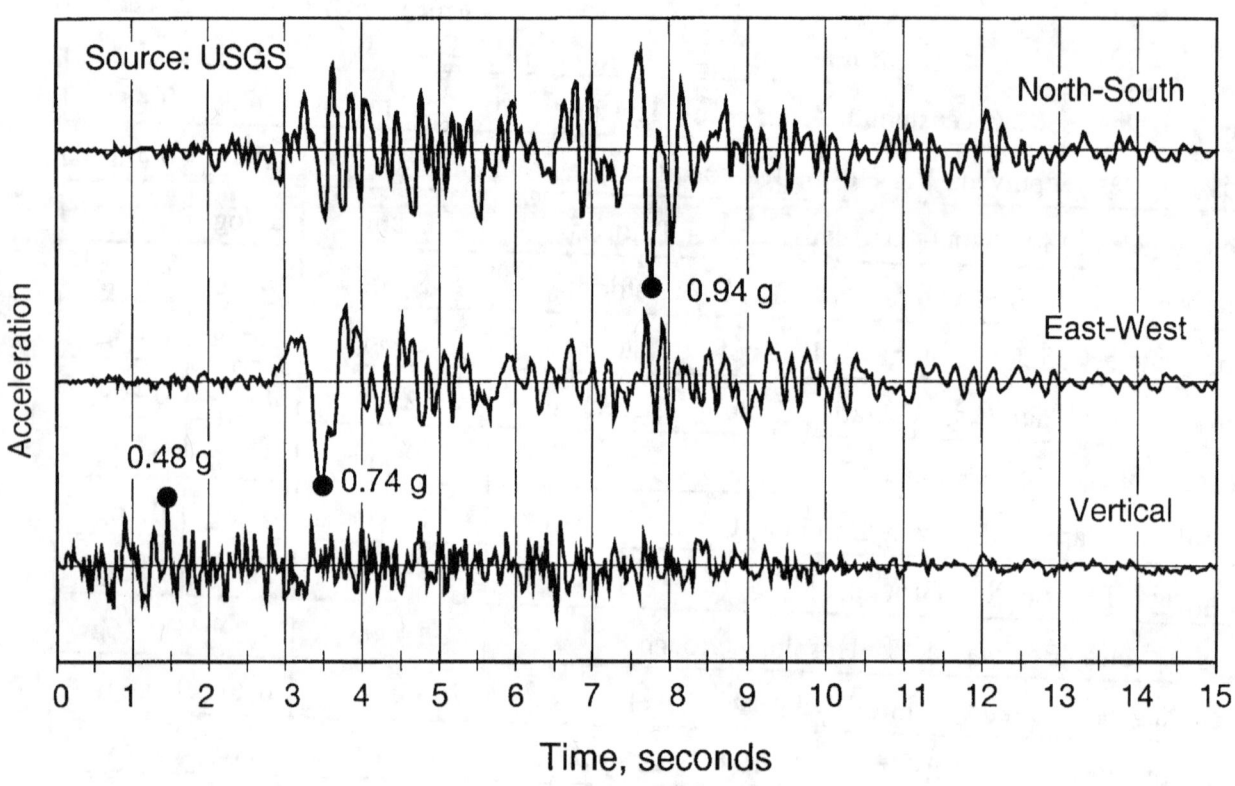

Figure 2.5 Accelerograph record from the grounds of the Sepulveda Veterans Affairs Hospital, 7 km from the epicenter.

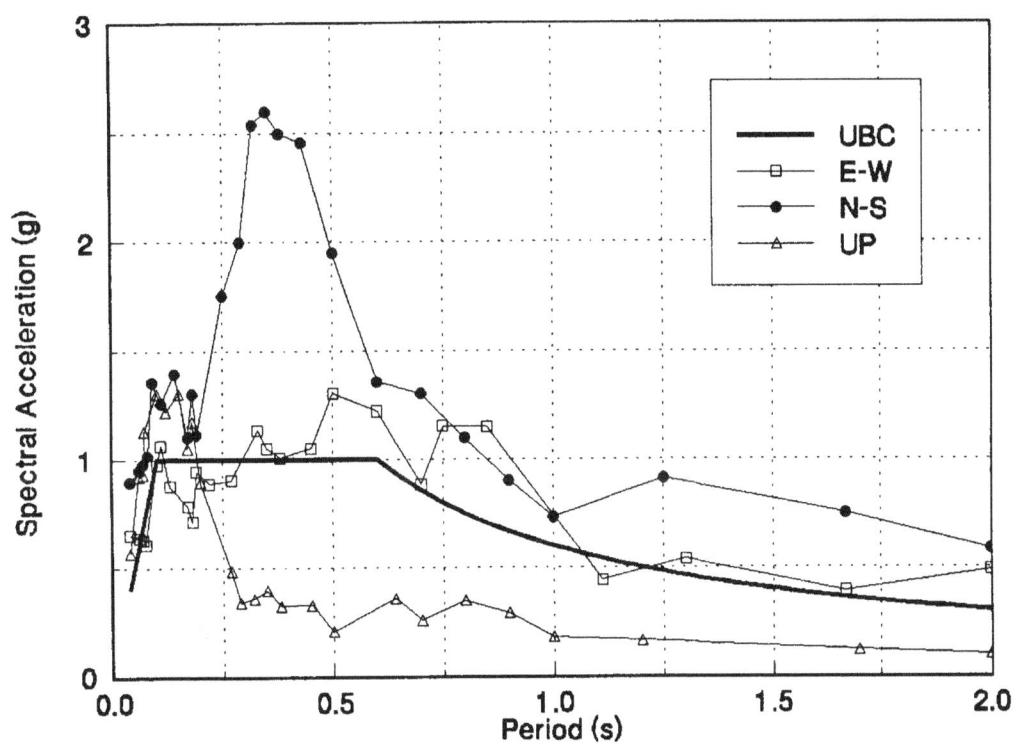

Figure 2.6 Response spectra, 5 percent damping, county hospital parking lot, Sylmar. (Source: Gary Hart, Hart Consultant Group; CSMIP records).

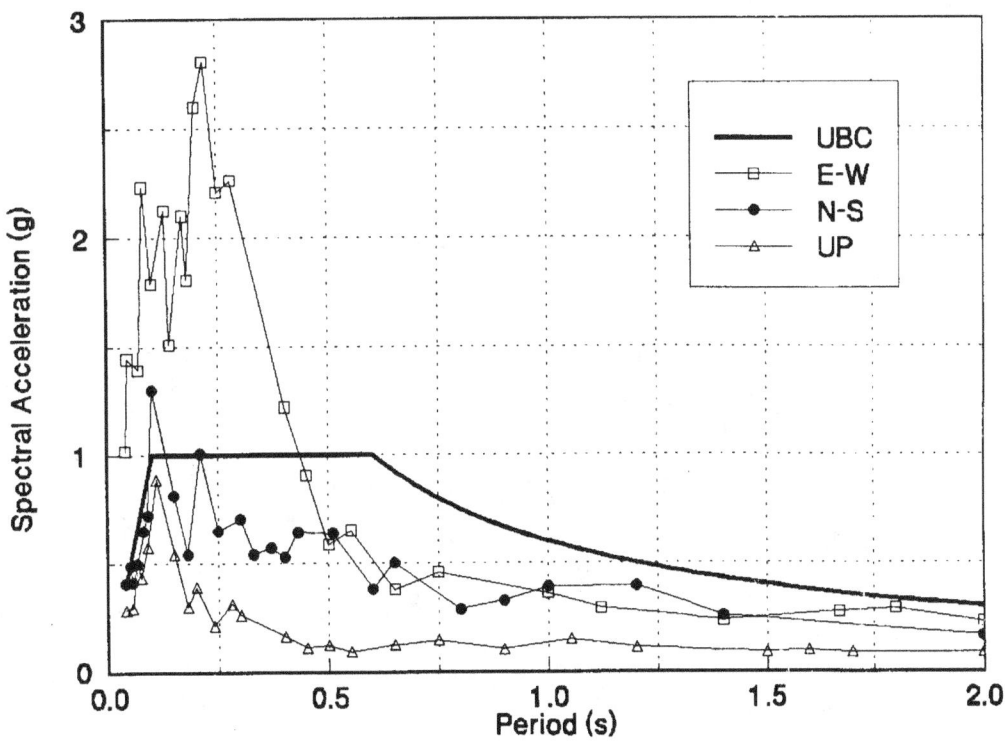

Figure 2.7 Response spectra, 5 percent damping, City Hall grounds, Santa Monica. (Source: Gary Hart, Hart Consultant Group; CSMIP records).

2.3 Geotechnical Aspects

The fracture of the thrust fault apparently did not reach the surface. No major surface faulting had been identified as of late March. Because of the developed nature of large portions of the affected area, surface distortions were not always readily visible, but had to be inferred from crushed curb stones, buckled sidewalks, and wrinkled pavement. In the undeveloped hills and canyons, fissures, slumps and other phenomena could be observed directly.

Landslides, rock slides and slope failures were the most visible geotechnical effect caused by the earthquake. Landslides along the Pacific coast in Santa Monica and Malibu damaged several buildings (fig. 2.8). Rockfalls in the Santa Monica, Santa Susana, and San Gabriel Mountains closed roads. Mulholland Drive in Sherman Oaks was temporarily closed because of the threat of slope failure.

Soil liquefaction was widely reported, but apparently caused little structural or agricultural damage. Sand boils (surface eruptions of fine sand and water due to sub-surface liquefaction) were reported along the Pacific coast from Mugu Lagoon to the north to the Port of Los Angeles in the south, and inland in the epicentral area, near the junctions of interstate highways 5 and 210 and 5 and 405 and in areas around Simi Valley northwest of the epicenter [2,5].

Liquefaction-related surface cracking and vertical offsets were reported at all sites where sand boils were observed. At other sites, such as the Jensen Filtration Plant in Sylmar and the nearby San Fernando Juvenile Hall, no sand boils were reported but lateral spreading and ground settlement indicate that liquefaction occurred. Minor breaks in water, sewer, and other pipe systems were widespread in areas of lateral spread and liquefaction.

Figure 2.8.   A landslide along the Pacific Coast Highway north of Santa Monica undermined the foundation of a house at the crest of the slope, bringing a portion of the house down.

2.4 Summary

Spectral analyses of the strong motion records generated by the quake should be correlated to damage states of constructed facilities to assess the need for modifying design requirements. It would be premature to call for an increase in design values based on the high peak accelerations recorded in this event without such an analysis. The maps that codes currently use to specify design values are not intended to be predictions of maximum ground accelerations. Instead they present "effective peak accelerations" related to the response characteristics of structures. Modern seismic design procedures are intended to produce structures with sufficient strength and ductility to retain their integrity when cyclically stressed beyond their elastic limits. Thus, buildings designed using modern code requirements should be able to resist transient accelerations that exceed the design acceleration. A thorough assessment of the good and poor performances of modern buildings relative to recorded ground motions will illuminate this issue.

CHAPTER 3

PERFORMANCE OF BUILDINGS

3.1 General Observations

The magnitude 6.8 Northridge earthquake provided the first full scale "test" of modern (post-1970's) seismic building codes in this country. For the first time, a large and varied population of buildings was subjected to ground shaking equal to or exceeding that recognized in modern codes for design. While the 1989 Loma Prieta earthquake south of San Francisco was of larger magnitude (7.1), the population of buildings in the epicentral region was relatively low. The ground acceleration caused by that event in the urban areas of San Francisco and Oakland was, in most cases, not as large as the design ground acceleration set for those locations by the building code [7]. The epicenter of the Northridge earthquake was located in a heavily populated urban/suburban area, the San Fernando Valley northwest of Los Angeles. In the epicentral region, most buildings experienced ground accelerations equal to or greater than that upon which the code design values are based.

The building damage caused by a magnitude 6.6 earthquake that occurred in the San Fernando Valley in 1971 prompted significant revisions to earthquake design requirements. The 1976 Uniform Building Code (UBC) [6] is often specified as a "benchmark" code that ushered in "modern" seismic design methods [8]. Comparisons of building response in the 1971 and 1994 quakes give some insight into the efficacy of earthquake mitigation practices that have been undertaken in the Los Angeles area in the intervening years.

3.1.1 The Goal of Building Code Adoption and Enforcement

The intent of building codes is to specify the minimum requirements needed for a structure to provide acceptable life-safety. For example, the 1990 National Building Code [9] states in Section 100.4,

> "This code shall be construed to secure its expressed intent, which is to insure public safety, health and welfare insofar as they are affected by building construction . . . "

The 1991 Uniform Building Code Section 102 states,

> "The purpose of this code is to provide minimum standards to safeguard life or limb, property and public welfare by regulating and controlling the design, construction, quality of materials, use and occupancy, location and maintenance of all buildings and structures."

The seismic provisions of the Uniform Building Code are based on *Recommended Lateral Force Requirements and Commentary* [10]. The commentary to that source document describes the intent of the seismic provisions thus:

> "Structures designed in conformance with these Recommendations should, in general, be able to:

17

1. Resist a minor level of earthquake ground motions without damage;
2. Resist a moderate level of earthquake ground motion without structural damage, but possibly experience some nonstructural damage;
3. Resist a major level of earthquake ground motion having an intensity equal to the strongest either experienced or forecast for the building site, without collapse, but possibly with some structural as well as nonstructural damage.

These expressed intents suggest that adherence to the minimum requirements of a building code is not sufficient in itself to prevent damage from an earthquake. However, the damage that does occur should not be life-threatening. Viewed in this light, the Northridge earthquake demonstrated the success of modern building codes. Of the 58 deaths attributed to the earthquake by the Los Angeles Department of the Coroner as of February 14, 1994, only 22 were caused by structural failures of buildings. The population of the three affected counties (Los Angeles, Ventura, and Orange) totals about nine million people; the number of earthquake deaths represents only a very small fraction of the affected population.

However, 80 000 to 125 000 people were made temporarily or permanently homeless because of damage to their homes and apartments. Schools, hospitals, offices, stores, and other commercial and industrial enterprises were forced to close due to damage, much of it nonstructural. Viewed in this light, the Northridge earthquake demonstrated the limitation of modern building codes. Because they do not include postearthquake serviceability requirements for most buildings, they do not ensure preservation of normal building function after an earthquake. Because they are not intended to prevent property damage in a large earthquake, economic losses can be high.

Greater levels of protection can be provided. Our understanding of earthquake motions and building responses is sufficient to allow buildings to be designed and constructed to be functional after a design-level quake. For example, the state of California requires special consideration of earthquake resistance for hospitals, with the intent of providing superior levels of protection of function as well as occupants. However, this added protection adds to the cost of design and construction. The question of how much protection to provide is not one for engineers to answer alone. All affected parts of society should participate in the weighing of costs against benefits to determine how much protection of property and function should be required by building codes.

In most circumstances, building codes cover only new construction or changes to existing construction. Rarely does a jurisdiction adopt and enforce a building code requirement that requires improvements to be made to existing buildings. For example, the city of Los Angeles established a requirement that all unreinforced masonry buildings larger than a specified size that were constructed prior to 1934 be assessed for seismic adequacy and, if necessary, rehabilitated. Requirements such as this can improve the seismic safety of a jurisdiction, but at potentially significant cost to specific building owners. While engineers can identify classes of seismically vulnerable buildings and develop requirements for upgrading those buildings, the decision to adopt and enforce such requirements is the responsibility of policymakers.

18

3.1.2 Behavior of Buildings

Within 10 km of the epicenter, unusually high ground accelerations were recorded. (See ch. 2.) The Los Angeles building code is based on the Uniform Building Code [6], which specifies a zone factor for the Los Angeles area which is equivalent to a design acceleration of 0.4g. In some locations the actual peak ground accelerations exceeded the specified design acceleration by a large margin. High vertical accelerations were also recorded. Current seismic design practices require consideration of vertical accelerations only in horizontal post-tensioned or cantilevered elements.

Buildings of all ages and types were damaged in the quake. However, it also should be noted that many buildings of all ages and types performed well. In the epicentral area, from the California State University, Northridge campus, to the Northridge Fashion Center mall, serious damage occurred. Several pockets of severe damage occurred at widely separated locations, such as downtown Santa Monica, along Ventura Boulevard in Sherman Oaks, downtown Glendale, and Hollywood Boulevard in Hollywood (fig. 3.1).

Accelerograms reveal that north-south shaking greatly exceeded east-west shaking in many locations [1]. The effects of this phenomenon were evident in the damage patterns, particularly in the epicentral area.

After an earthquake, the safety of damaged buildings must be assessed. All jurisdictions in the affected area used a system of red, yellow and green "tags" to indicate the condition of a damaged building as assessed by an official inspector. Red tags indicate a building is unsafe and presents an extreme hazard. No one may enter a building once it has been posted with a red tag. Yellow tagged buildings may be entered, but not reoccupied. In buildings posted with a green tag, the inspector found the level of damage would not pose a threat to life-safety; entry and use of these buildings is not restricted [11].

A red tag does not automatically mean a building will be demolished. Jurisdictions typically use red tags to denote buildings classified as a "public nuisance". In the city of Los Angeles, owners of red tagged buildings must complete repairs within thirty days or face demolition by city-hired contractors (Los Angeles Times, March 25, 1994). Many red-tagged buildings are repaired. All red and yellow-tagged buildings must be repaired to the satisfaction of the local jurisdiction before they can be reoccupied.

In Los Angeles alone, over 60 000 buildings were damaged to some degree and required inspection. Of these, 2076 were red-tagged as of early March, consisting of 1608 residential, 459 commercial, and 9 mixed-use buildings [2]. Yellow tags were issued to over 7000 buildings. The total number of red-tagged buildings throughout the affected area is estimated to be about 3000 [2]. The distribution of red and yellow-tagged buildings in the affected area is shown in Figure 3.2.

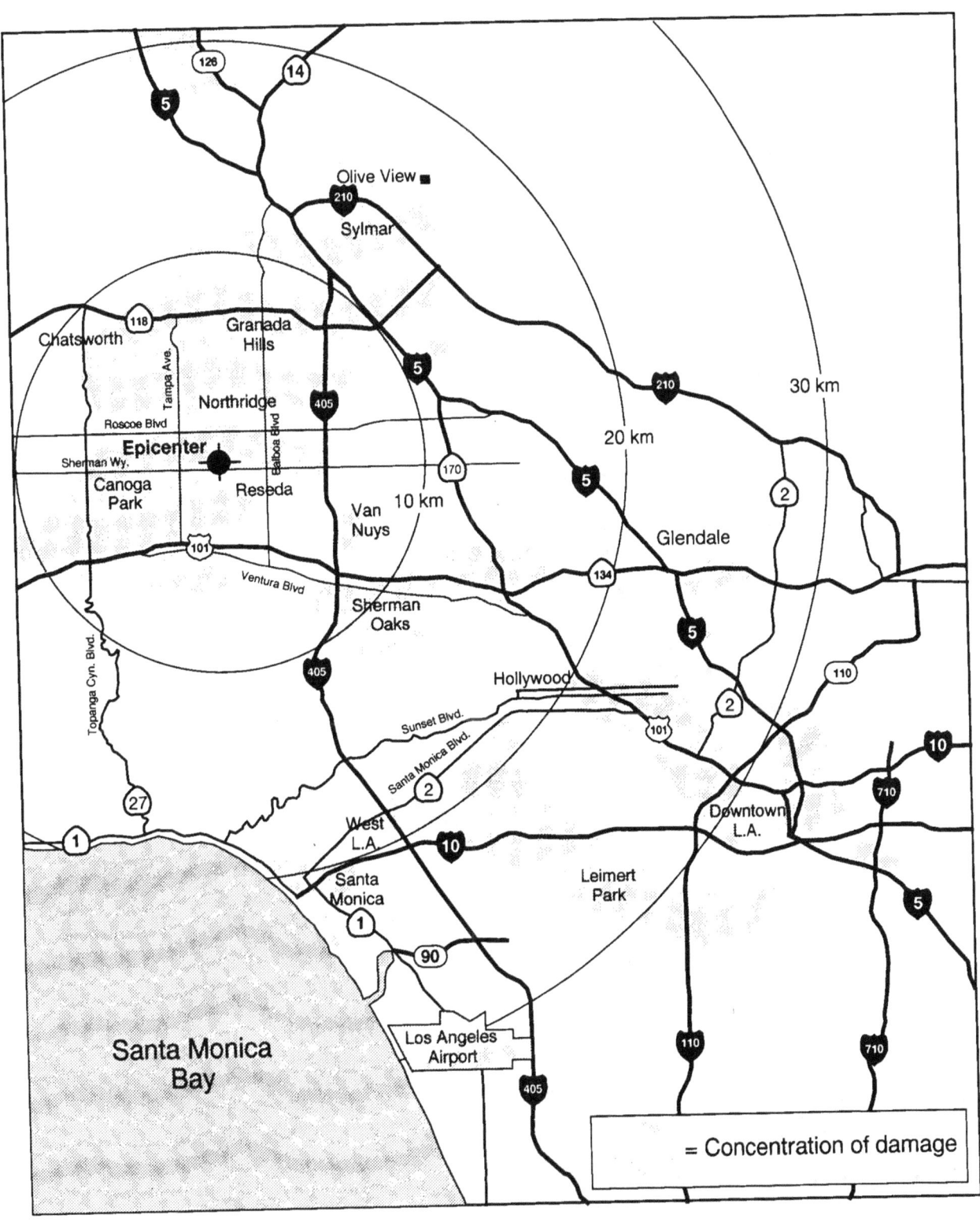

Figure 3.1. Serious damage to buildings caused by the magnitude 6.8 Northridge earthquake was widespread, but, outside of the epicentral area, seriously damaged buildings tended to occur in pockets.

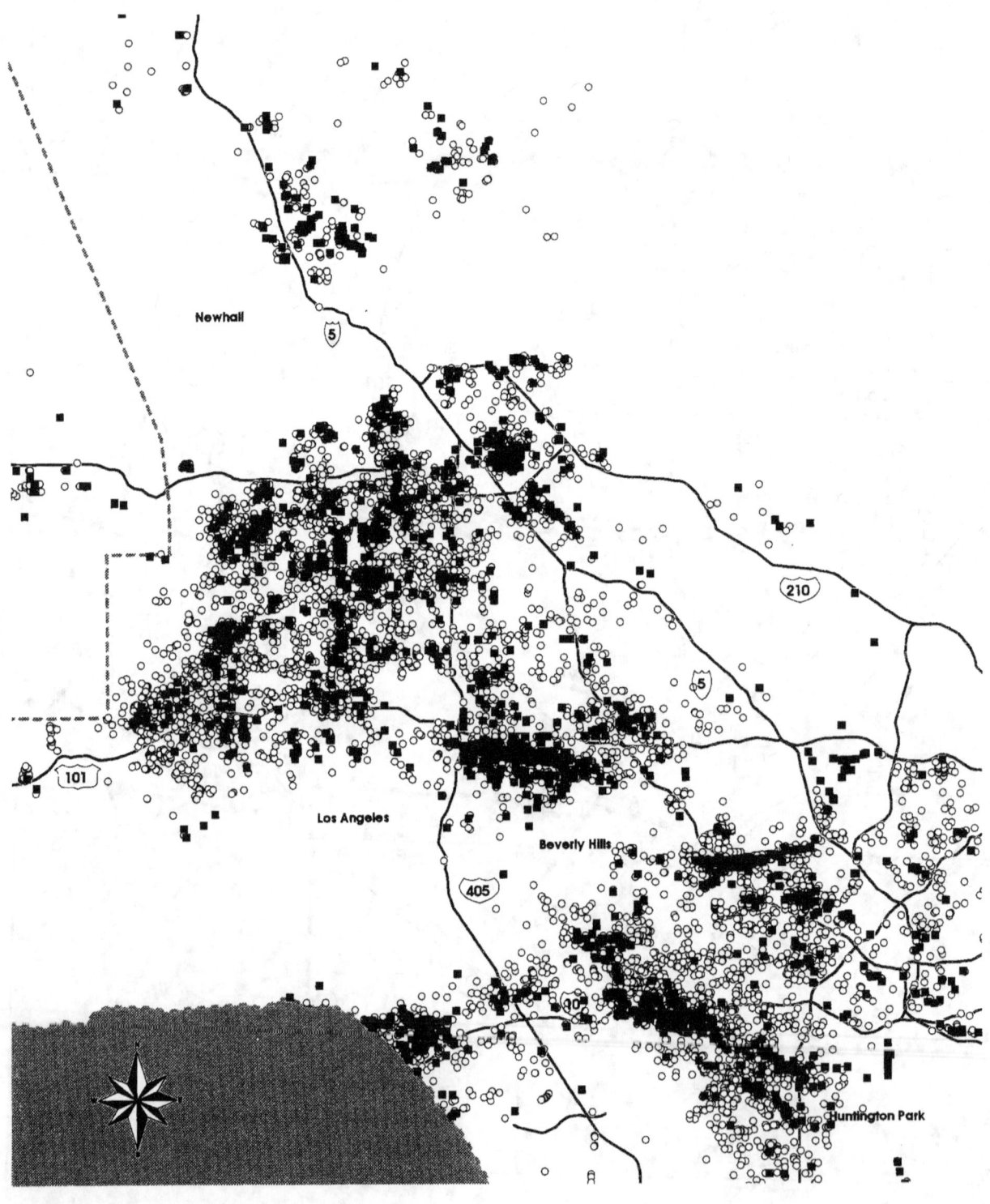

Figure 3.2.   Solid squares indicate locations of red-tagged buildings.   Open circles indicate
yellow-tagged buildings.   (Source: Integration Technologies)

21

3.2 Single and Multi-Family Residences

3.2.1 Low-Rise Apartment Buildings

Collapses in a single apartment complex caused sixteen of the twenty-two deaths related to building failures [12]. The Northridge Meadows complex, constructed in 1972 (Los Angeles Times, January 19, 1994), consisted of several three-story wood-frame buildings, arrayed around courtyards on two sides of a mid-block alley. About half of the units had open spaces for parking on the street level. Typically these were around the perimeter of the complex. Most of the interior courtyard-facing units had living space at the ground level rather than parking. About half of the buildings in the complex collapsed. In all of the collapses, the first story gave way while the second and third stories remained largely intact. The 16 people killed were in first story apartments. All the buildings in the complex suffered some damage (figs. 3.3 and 3.4).

The buildings were predominantly wood-frame, with wire mesh and stucco walls. Rows of steel pipe columns supported the upper stories along the building perimeter between parking bays (fig. 3.5). Transverse walls were typically spaced about every three parking bays. Longitudinal walls separated the parking areas from first story living spaces. The wire mesh and stucco coating on these walls provided insufficient resistance to the lateral earthquake forces generated by this earthquake.

The upper stories of the collapsed buildings were displaced laterally and in some cases came to rest offset by as much as three meters from their original locations. The steel pipe columns, which hinged at their bases, apparently controlled the distance of the offset as they bent to the ground under the load of the building above (fig. 3.6). Collapses occurred in buildings aligned longitudinally east-west as well as those aligned north-south. At the southeast end of the complex, some building portions collapsed to the north, and other portions collapsed to the south, which indicates that no one extreme pulse of energy brought all the buildings down.

The Northridge Meadows building configuration, two stories of living space in a long, narrow building above one level of parking, is common in the San Fernando Valley. Many buildings of this type sustained serious damage, and some collapsed. The typical apartment building collapses occurred in buildings which had stiff, box-like upper stories supported by few walls and flexible pipe columns in the parking areas below. Typical damage included racking of the first story (fig. 3.7), horizontal cracks at the foundation-first floor interface (fig. 3.8), and diagonal cracking in stucco at corners of windows (fig. 3.9).

The Northridge Meadows apartment buildings and many others that suffered serious damage were built in the late 1960's or early 1970's, when use of stucco for seismic resistance in low-rise buildings was not uncommon. Current codes require that when stucco is used for earthquake resistance in areas of high seismicity, the entire building be designed to resist 1.33 times the earthquake force that is required in design of a plywood-sheathed building [6]. This requirement effectively eliminates the use of stucco as a lateral force resisting element due to economic concerns. The 1970 Uniform Building Code did not have a similar requirement.

A more unusual collapse occurred in an apartment building of more recent vintage with the entire first story used for parking, located on Sherman Way in Sepulveda. In this building, the first story parking area was open only on the transverse ends. Concrete block walls formed the longitudinal walls at the first story and a row of concrete columns supported the mid-span of the flat plate concrete floor slab above. The two stories of living space over the parking level were wood-framed with a stucco facade. The entire line of mid-span concrete columns failed. The two halves of the upper stories settled in towards the middle (figs. 3.10 and 3.11), essentially destroying the structure.

Damage to low-rise unreinforced masonry apartment buildings was similar to damage to unreinforced masonry commercial buildings, as discussed in section 3.3.3.

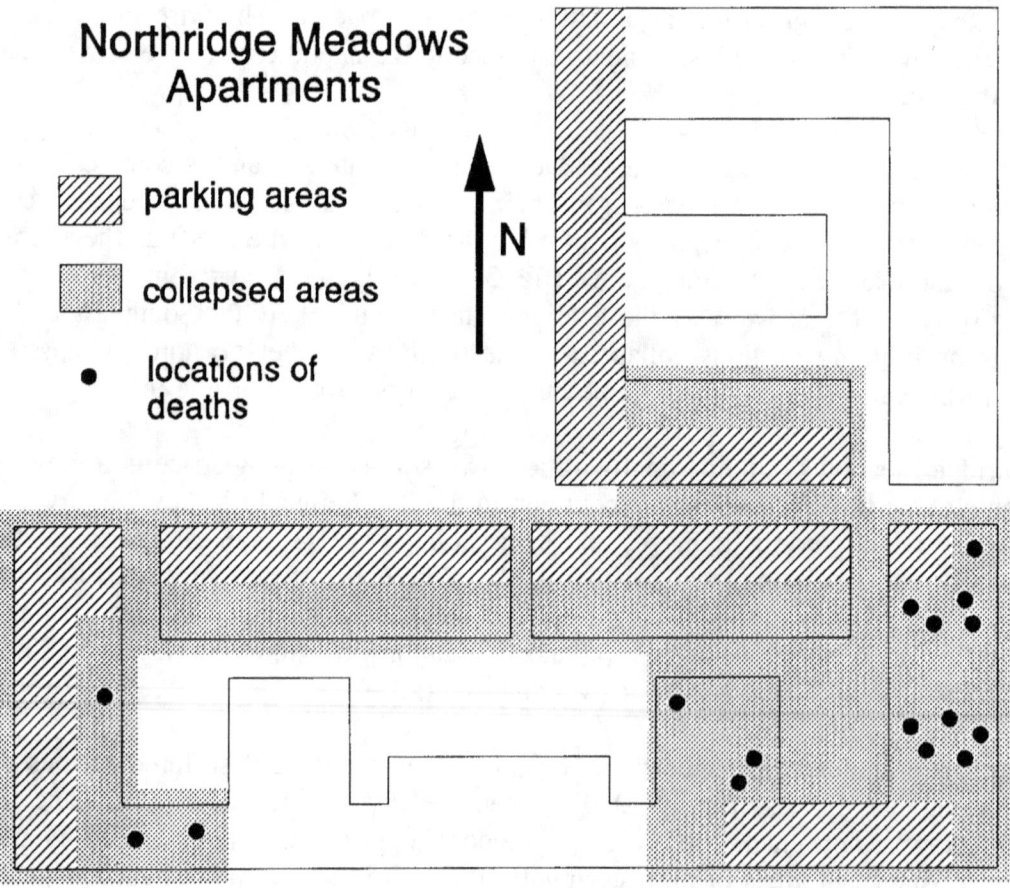

Figure 3.3.   This plan of the Northridge Meadows apartment complex shows the distribution of parking and living spaces at the first level, and locations of deaths (source: Los Angeles Times, January 24, 1994). The shaded areas indicate the portions of the complex which collapsed.

Figure 3.4. At the Northridge Meadows apartment complex near the epicenter the first story in several of the buildings collapsed, killing sixteen people. The second and third stories remained essentially intact. Large portions of the first story in these buildings were open space for parking. This type of collapse occurred in a significant number of similar apartment buildings throughout the affected area.

Figure 3.5. Steel pipe columns between parking bays supported the upper stories of the Northridge Meadows apartment buildings. Few of the buildings in the north half of the complex collapsed, but all were damaged.

Figure 3.6. At Northridge Meadows, the first story steel pipe columns generally hinged near their bases but retained their length, controlling the displacement of the upper stories.

Figure 3.7. Racking, or leaning, of open first story parking areas was a common feature of damaged two and three-story apartment buildings.

Figure 3.8. Horizontal cracks at the interface of the foundation wall (usually concrete) and the first story (typically wood-framed with stucco facade) were often seen in damaged low-rise apartment buildings.

Figure 3.9. Typical damage in to low-rise apartment buildings included diagonal cracks in the stucco facade at the corners of windows and other openings.

Figure 3.10.   The central row of concrete first-story columns in a three story apartment building on Sherman Way in Van Nuys collapsed, causing the wood-framed upper stories to settle inward.

Figure 3.11.   This overhead view of the partially-collapsed apartment building on Sherman Way shows the solid concrete masonry block perimeter walls along the longitudinal axis of the building. Access to the first story parking was limited to the transverse ends of the building. When the row of interior columns failed, both sides of the building settled in towards the middle.

3.2.2 High-Rise Apartment Buildings and Hotels

Champagne Towers on Ocean Avenue in Santa Monica, a 16-story concrete apartment building, suffered serious damage. The condition of this building illustrates two classic examples of earthquake damage: damaged coupling beams between linked shear walls and shear failure of unintentionally short columns.

The transverse end walls are pierced by a single vertical row of window openings. The wall segments between the windows act as coupling beams linking the wall segments on either side. These coupling beams suffered serious diagonal cracking, increasing in severity from top to bottom of the building (fig. 3.12).

In the longitudinal direction, the lateral-force resistance is apparently provided by concrete moment frames. The front of the building shows no sign of damage (fig. 3.13). At the back, the columns and transverse wall ends are diagonally cracked (fig. 3.14). Doors in the transverse walls and open passageways connect the spaces behind these cracked columns in the middle third of the building (fig. 3.15). The solid infill railings which rise to about mid-height of the columns create an unintentional "short-column" effect. The solid railings made the bottom half of each column extremely rigid. This forced the top half of the column to accommodate all of the differential movement between stories. These shortened columns, apparently not detailed to accommodate the motion, failed in shear. At the front of the building, metal pipe railings are provided at the balconies rather than solid infill, as at the back. This may partially explain why there is no apparent damage at the front of the building.

The high-rise concrete apartment buildings directly adjacent to Champagne Towers were also damaged, but to a lesser extent. Diagonal cracks in the facade of the building to the north were already being repaired four days after the quake.

Several mid to high-rise concrete hotels in the Van Nuys area were damaged. Of particular interest is the seven-story Holiday Inn. The building has end shear walls in the transverse direction and a perimeter concrete moment resisting frame in the longitudinal direction. Columns in the lower two stories were damaged in the 1971 San Fernando earthquake. These were subsequently repaired with epoxy injection and strengthened. Damage caused by the 1994 quake was concentrated at the top of the fourth-floor columns (fig. 3.16). This seems to suggest that the dynamic characteristics of the building were changed due to the rehabilitation work in 1971. As a result, damage appears to have occurred in concrete members which did not sustain damage in the 1971 event. This building was instrumented with strong-motion recorders, and records are available from both the 1971 and 1994 quakes.

Figure 3.12. Champagne Towers apartment building in Santa Monica suffered a classic form of earthquake damage: shear failure of the coupling beams between linked shear walls at the transverse end of the building.

Figure 3.13. The front of the 16-story Champagne Towers building had no apparent damage. Note the steel pipe railings at the balconies.

Figure 3.14. The back of the Champagne Towers building was badly damaged. The railings here are solid infill, which effectively stiffen the lower half of the columns. The shortened upper half of the columns were forced to accommodate all the displacement, and they failed in shear.

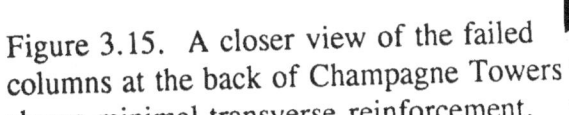

Figure 3.15. A closer view of the failed columns at the back of Champagne Towers shows minimal transverse reinforcement.

Figure 3.16.   The bottom two stories of the concrete frame Holiday Inn in Van Nuys were damaged in the 1971 San Fernando quake and subsequently repaired. In the 1994 Northridge quake, damage was concentrated at the top of the fourth floor columns.

3.2.3 Single Family Dwellings

Only a handful of single-family homes collapsed. One collapse was caused by a landslide which undermined the foundation of a house overlooking the Pacific Coast Highway north of Santa Monica. (See ch. 2.) A landslide in Malibu damaged several buildings at the foot of the slope. In Sherman Oaks, two houses collapsed down steep hillside sites. Three people were killed in these failures. The team did not observe any collapse of a single-family home that was unrelated to a slope failure or hillside site.

The most common and easily visible damage to single family homes was damaged and collapsed masonry chimneys (fig. 3.17). In some cases, the chimney fell onto and through the roof. Cracked stucco, fallen roof tiles, and racked garage door openings were visible throughout the affected area. Some houses shifted on their foundations. In the epicentral area, damage to concrete masonry fences at the edges of lots was almost universal (fig. 3.18). Piles of debris outside many homes attested to widespread interior nonstructural and contents damage.

3.2.4 Manufactured Housing

The vulnerability of mobile homes to earthquake ground shaking was demonstrated once again by the Northridge earthquake. For example, in a trailer park near the epicenter, at the intersection of Nordhoff Street and Tampa Avenue, nearly every home had moved on its supports. These types of homes are usually supported on small concrete and metal base supports (figs. 3.19, 3.20, and 3.21). These supports provide little resistance to lateral movements, and toppled during the quake (fig. 3.22). The identical failure was observed in the 1971 San Fernando earthquake. It is clear that no improvements in the practice of supporting manufactured homes adequately against lateral loads have been made during the past twenty-three years.

In some cases, the metal base supports were braced with small steel angle members. However, they were not adequately fastened to the supports and did not prevent the supports from rocking.

Chapter 6 discusses fire ignition and spread in several trailer park communities.

Figure 3.17.   Failure of masonry chimneys was common.

Figure 3.18.   Damage to masonry privacy fences was ubiquitous. Many of these fences were tall enough to have been a serious threat to passersby when they failed. Luckily, due to the early morning hour of the quake, yards and sidewalks were essentially deserted.

Figure 3.19. Damage to manufactured homes caused by collapsed supports was common.

Figure 3.20. Small concrete base supports are a common foundation system used to support manufactured housing. This type of system provided little resistance to lateral forces.

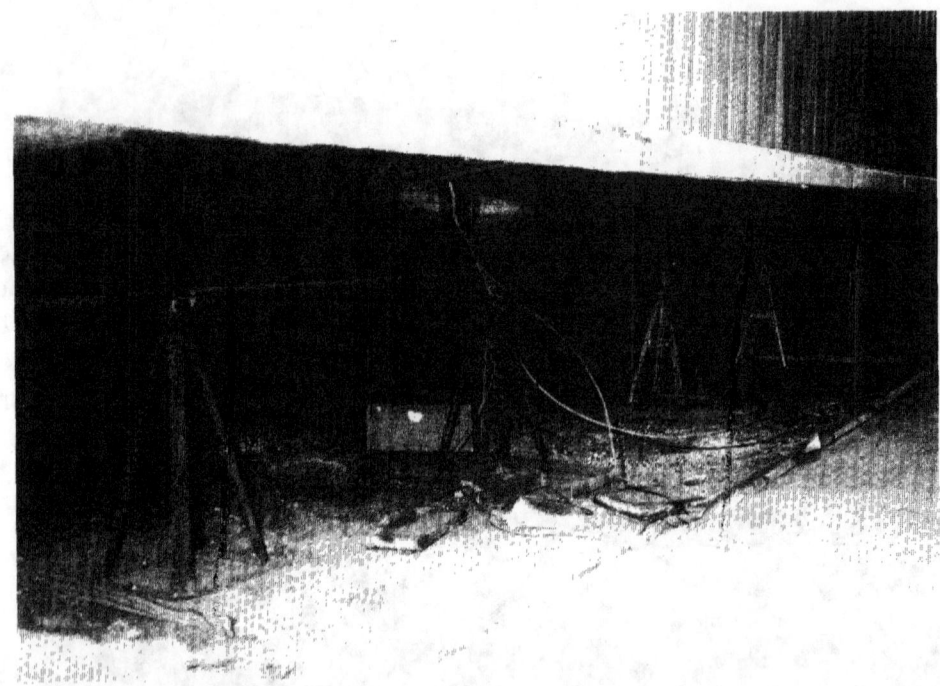

Figure 3.21.   Another foundation system used for manufactured housing consists of supports constructed of small metal angles.

Figure 3.22.   The metal supports under many homes tipped over, bringing down the houses above.

3.3 Commercial and Institutional Buildings

3.3.1 Hospitals and Medical Facilities

Following the 1971 San Fernando earthquake, California enacted the California Hospital Act, which attempted to improve the earthquake resistance of California hospitals by mandating enhanced levels of design and construction. (The Hospital Act does not apply to convalescent homes, nursing homes, or medical office buildings, only to acute-care facilities.) Despite these strict requirements, two hospitals constructed after 1971 were inoperable after the earthquake: the Holy Cross Medical Center and the Olive View Medical Center. Neither of the closures was due to structural damage [2].

At both Holy Cross and Olive View, the original hospitals at the sites were badly damaged in the 1971 San Fernando earthquake. The damaged structures were demolished and new facilities constructed following the requirements of the Hospital Act. At both facilities, the structural systems performed very well in the 1994 quake. At Olive View, damage to the sprinkler and chilled water systems made the building temporarily unusable. Several air handling units on the roof came off their supports. At Holy Cross, damage to the air handling system forced the closure. A large portion of the facade of the roof-enclosure was detached when it was struck by the damaged fan. The facility also suffered water damage from broken sprinklers and other piping. These failures illustrate the need for all systems within critical facilities, not just the structural system, to be sufficiently earthquake-resistant.

St. John's Hospital in Santa Monica was closed due to structural damage. The seven-story northwest wing, which was about fifty years old, had severe diagonal cracks in the piers between the windows (figs. 3.23 and 3.24). In the circa-1960's southeast wing, horizontal construction-joint cracks were visible in the exterior walls.

Many buildings had significant amounts of damage in the few blocks surrounding the St. John's Hospital complex. The concrete parking garage at the northwest end of the complex was damaged; the exterior facade panels had diagonal cracks across each panel, and crushed toes (fig. 3.25). To the southeast, a six-story concrete office building had cracked shear walls and broken glass. Several of the columns in this building were also cracked.

To the southwest, the Bay Vista Health Care Center, a three-story concrete frame convalescent home with parking space in the back half of the first story, was closed because of damage. At the front of the building, earthquake forces had shifted the exterior facade relative to the concrete foundation wall below, crushing the toe of the facade and spalling the corner of the foundation wall (fig. 3.26). The second-story exterior facade panel over the south opening to the garage fell to the alley below. Two rectangular concrete piers in the garage area had diagonal cracking, but did not spall significantly. Smaller square columns on the perimeter of the garage area spalled at the top, revealing limited transverse reinforcement in the columns. At the first floor parking area, concrete block infill walls laid in stack bond had diagonal cracks running through the masonry units. Infill walls laid in running bond lost the top row of units but did not crack diagonally.

The Berkley East Convalescent Hospital, directly northwest of the St. John's Hospital complex, was also closed due to damage. The five-story building, constructed in the 1969, has an interior concrete frame with shear walls, and exterior walls of reinforced clay masonry. In the basement level parking area, none of the concrete slabs, columns, or shear walls showed any significant cracking or spalling. The exterior masonry walls, constructed of two wythes of brick masonry with a fully-grouted and reinforced space between them, were heavily damaged (fig. 3.27). The walls on the southeast and northeast sides of the building had short perpendicular wing walls separating balconies. The ends of many of these walls spalled at the first story, often at locations of lap splices of reinforcement at the wall ends (fig. 3.28). Between the wing walls, the masonry above the windows had diagonal cracks. The northwest and southwest walls did not have wing walls. The northwest wall suffered severe diagonal cracking and dislodging of bricks in the piers between the first story windows. The southwest wall, which had fewer windows, was not as badly damaged.

The Granada Hills Community Hospital on Balboa Avenue is directly adjacent to the five-story Kaiser Permanente office building that collapsed. (See section 3.3.4 for a description of the Kaiser Permanente building.) There was no evidence of structural damage to this three-story building. The hospital continued to operate, despite loss of water and heat (Los Angeles Times, January 19, 1994). An emergency care center was established in the parking lot.

Figure 3.23.   The seven-story northwest wing of St. John's hospital in Santa Monica experienced severe X-cracking in the piers between the second story windows.

Figure 3.24.   The transverse reinforcement in the St. John's hospital window piers was spaced at about 150-200 mm on center with 90° hooks at the ends, typical for construction of its age (about 50 years old).

Figure 3.25. The concrete facade panels of the St. John's hospital parking garage had diagonal cracks and crushed toes.

Figure 3.26. The Bay Vista Health Care Center was closed due to damage. Differential movement between the building and its base was indicated by the crack at the foundation line. The corner of the concrete foundation wall spalled, apparently due to crushing. A facade panel over the garage opening was dislodged.

Figure 3.27. The facade of the five-story Berkley Convalescent Hospital directly adjacent to the St. John's Hospital complex consisted of two wythes of brick masonry with a reinforced and grouted space between. In some places, all three layers of this facade were destroyed along lines of diagonal cracking. The facility was evacuated.

Figure 3.28. Two faces of the Berkley Convalescent Hospital had wing walls separating balconies. The ends of these wing walls spalled at the lower stories.

40

3.3.2 Commercial Buildings

The collapse of large portions of the roof and floors of the three-story concrete Bullock's department store at the Northridge Fashion Center mall could have caused more deaths than any other single building failure in this earthquake. Many multi-story columns were left intact as the concrete slab floors and roof fell on top of each other to the basement, presumably due to punching shear failure of the slabs. The still-standing columns showed no evidence that slab reinforcement had been continuous through the columns (fig. 3.29). At the roof level, about a half meter of the column bar ends were bent over into the slab. The original building was extremely irregular, with a non-rectilinear vertical profile (fig. 3.30). Even in extremely regular buildings, this type of construction, which depends on the slab-column connection for moment-frame action, is vulnerable to damage from earthquake forces.

Other stores at the Northridge Fashion Center were damaged, but none collapsed. The three-story Broadway, north and west of Bullock's, had horizontal cracks in the clay masonry facade at each floor level, and crushing and spalling at the building corners at each floor level. The soffits were also cracked (fig. 3.31). The Robinsons-May department store at the west side of the mall had almost no visible exterior damage. Sears, to the south, lost facade and cornice panels. Three of the parking garages at the Northridge Fashion Center were damaged. These are discussed in section 3.4.

The area around the Northridge Fashion Center showed evidence of having been severely shaken. Significant damage of many types occurred. South of the Northridge Fashion Center, several single story retail structures were damaged; at least one, the Wherehouse, collapsed (fig. 3.32).

In the same area, the entire south wall of the concrete tilt-up Levitz furniture store fell away from the building to the south (fig. 3.33). In tilt-up construction, the concrete walls are formed and poured on the ground and, after the concrete cures, rotated into their final erect position. The remains of the damaged roof of the Levitz store, a plywood diaphragm, appeared to be supported by the top of the racks holding furniture.

To the south of the Levitz store/warehouse is a concrete stream channel and a set of railroad tracks. A freight train derailed during the earthquake directly behind the Levitz, but neither incident appeared to have caused the other. The embankments of a city street overpass to the west of the Levitz store settled by about 350 mm. The overpass had to be closed.

To the south of the railroad tracks and channelized stream, damage fell off dramatically. A tilt-up concrete building to the west showed no evidence of damage. No structural damage was visible in the modern single-story, reinforced masonry, garage-fronted commercial buildings (fig. 3.34), neither in the parapets nor the piers around the garage openings, doors, or windows. Clean-up activities in progress suggested that damage did occur to contents of these buildings.

Numerous two and three-story buildings at the Topanga Plaza mall on the east side of Topanga Canyon Boulevard in Canoga Park suffered damage to their facades, but none collapsed. A few blocks to the north, the two story Chatsworth Post Office was closed due to damage: an exterior facade panel had become detached and interior ceiling panels had fallen (fig. 3.35). Mail was being collected in the parking lot.

Figure 3.29. A portion of the concrete waffle slab roof and the interior floor slabs at the Bullock's department store at the Northridge Fashion Center mall fell to the basement, leaving many of the columns standing. No reinforcing steel can be seen in the remaining columns that would have connected the columns to the floor slabs.

Figure 3.30. The Bullock's department store had an extremely irregular vertical geometry. At the northeast end it was shaped like a truncated pyramid.

Figure 3.31. The Broadway department store at the Northridge Fashion Center had horizontal cracks in the facade and spalled corners at each floor level, and cracks in the soffit.

Figure 3.32. Many commercial buildings were damaged in the blocks south of the Northridge Fashion Center. The single-story Wherehouse collapsed completely.

Figure 3.33.   The south wall of the concrete tilt-up Levitz furniture store/warehouse south of the Northridge Fashion Center fell away from the building into the alley and stream channel. The damaged roof was being supported by the racks of furniture. On the south side of the stream channel a freight train derailed during the earthquake. That clean-up effort was still underway three days after the quake.

Figure 3.34.   The single-story modern masonry commercial buildings directly south of the damaged Levitz furniture store and train derailment were apparently undamaged. All parapets and piers between garage openings appeared intact.

Figure 3.35.   The Chatsworth Post Office was closed due to damage. Mail was being collected in the parking lot.

Figure 3.36.   Damage to unreinforced masonry buildings, even those that had been rehabilitated, was common. Upper stories and corners were particularly vulnerable to damage. The rows of light-colored diamonds on the face of this building are the end plates of through-bolts used to connect the wall to the floor joists, a typical rehabilitation technique. The remains of parapet braces can be seen on the roof.

46

3.3.3 Unreinforced Masonry Buildings

Modern masonry construction in regions of high seismicity provides the ductility necessary for the building to survive earthquake shaking by incorporating reinforcing steel and fully grouting all the void spaces. This approach to masonry construction, known as reinforced masonry, began to be used in California in 1934, after dramatic building failures caused by the 1933 Long Beach quake demonstrated the vulnerability of unreinforced masonry.

Many pre-1934 unreinforced masonry buildings still exist in the Los Angeles area. The earthquake resistance of these buildings can be improved through rehabilitation. Most rehabilitation schemes use through-bolts and face plates to connect the wood floor and roof diaphragms to the masonry walls. These bolts are clearly visible on the exterior of a building, simplifying identification of rehabilitated structures. Los Angeles has mandatory rehabilitation requirements for unreinforced masonry buildings constructed prior to 1934. One and two-family dwellings and small apartment buildings are exempted, so the statute affects primarily commercial buildings. These rehabilitation requirements, known as Division 88, establish criteria for "complete" strengthening, which, in addition to through-bolts, may require adding interior wood shear wall partitions, incorporating new posts or other supplemental vertical load resisting elements, infilling openings, or increasing wall thicknesses [13]. From exterior inspection, it is not possible to tell whether a rehabilitation is "complete."

The business districts in Santa Monica and along Hollywood Boulevard in Los Angeles both have significant populations of one to four-story commercial buildings of unreinforced masonry. While Los Angeles has a mandated rehabilitation requirement for these types of structures, Santa Monica does not. Nevertheless, rows of through-bolts can be seen on most unreinforced masonry buildings in Santa Monica. Despite rehabilitation, many of the unreinforced masonry buildings in Santa Monica and in Hollywood were badly damaged.

As a life-safety measure, rehabilitation was somewhat successful in the Northridge earthquake; there were no complete collapses and no deaths of occupants. There were also no deaths or injuries on the sidewalks adjoining the damaged unreinforced masonry buildings, but this was due only to the early morning hour. Rehabilitation was not successful at preventing damage. Serious damage occurred to many structures. Portions of buildings disintegrated; top stories and corners were particularly vulnerable (figs. 3.36, 3.37, and 3.38). Common damage included loss of significant areas of wall between rows of through-bolts. In some instances, only a single wythe was dislodged (fig. 3.39); in others the entire thickness of the wall crumbled (fig. 3.40). The same types of damage to rehabilitated buildings were noted following the 1987 Whittier Narrows earthquake and the 1989 Loma Prieta earthquake [7, 14]. In the 1989 Loma Prieta earthquake, a significant portion of the people killed by building failures were outside unreinforced masonry structures that lost portions of walls [7].

Figure 3.37.   The corner of this rehabilitated unreinforced masonry apartment building in East Hollywood crumbled on all four stories.

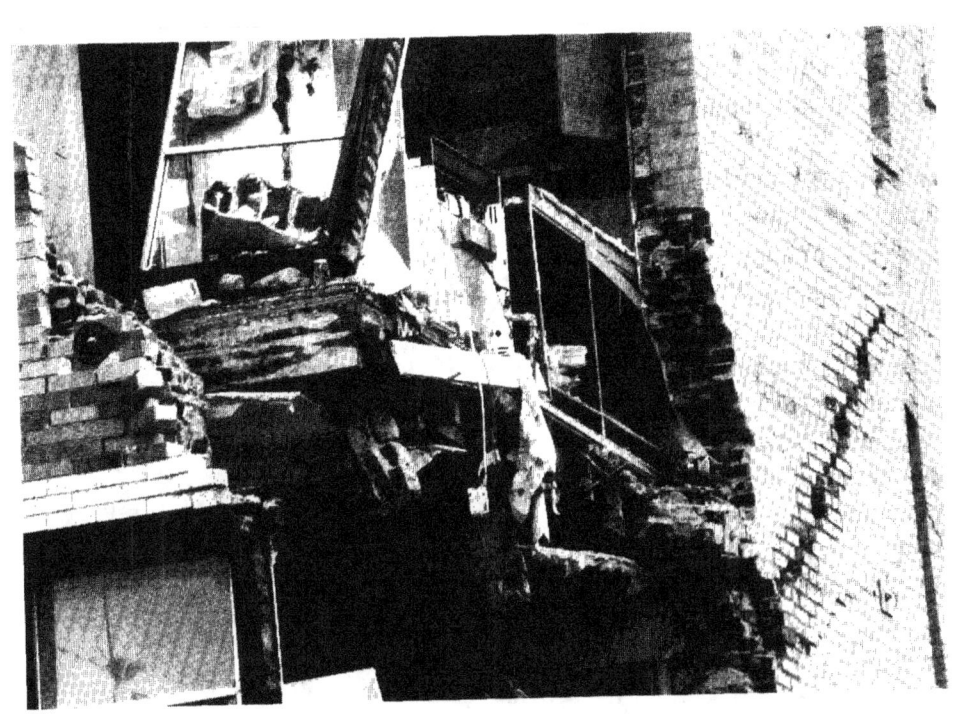

Figure 3.38.   A close-up view of the third-story floor diaphragm of the building picture above shows (lower right) a rehabilitation bolt still holding a few bricks to the floor joists, after all the walls on three out of four sides of the bolts had disintegrated.

Figure 3.39.　　Only the exterior wythe of brick peeled off of this rehabilitated unreinforced masonry building in Santa Monica.

Figure 3.40.　　In other rehabilitated unreinforced masonry buildings, such as this two story structure in Hollywood, entire wall thicknesses were lost between rows of through-bolts.

3.3.4 Office Buildings

The most spectacular damage to office buildings occurred in mid-rise structures: the five-story Kaiser Permanente office building on Balboa Avenue, the six-story Barrington Building on Olympic Boulevard, and the five-story Digital office building on Sherman Way.

The concrete frame Kaiser Permanente office building on Balboa Boulevard in Granada Hills was badly damaged. The second story columns disintegrated, causing the upper stories to collapse onto the first story, which remained intact (fig. 3.41). At the ends of the building, damage to the frame caused partial collapses, but the mid-section of the building remained intact. The apparently nonstructural end walls became detached at both ends of the building and slid to the ground (figs. 3.42 and 3.43). The failure of these end walls may have contributed to the damage to the frame at the ends of the building.

The bare frame exposed by the damage suggests that the buildings had a strong-beam/weak-column configuration (fig. 3.44). The damage appears to have initiated at the joints. At the damaged ends, the beams and columns remained essentially intact, but the joints disintegrated.

The L-shaped concrete frame Barrington Building in West Los Angeles also had damage concentrated in the second story columns (fig. 3.45). In this building, the horizontal architectural panels stiffened the lower half of the columns at each story, creating a short-column effect. The effectively shortened columns failed in shear between the windows, creating a pattern of X-cracking in the columns that diminished in severity towards the top (fig. 3.46). At the second story, the cracking was severe enough to cause a loss of vertical-load-carrying capacity; the bulging window frames indicate about a 50 to 100 mm reduction in height (fig. 3.47). The building was demolished within a few days of the quake.

The column-shortening effect of the infill panels was apparently not considered in the design. Where column reinforcing was exposed, transverse bars of undeformed steel spaced at about 300 mm on center could be seen (fig. 3.48), not sufficient to provide confinement of the concrete in a region of high shear.

A five-story steel and concrete office building occupied by the Digital Equipment Corporation on Sherman Way lost the enclosing masonry end wall and stair tower (fig. 3.49) on the east side of the building. The corresponding wall on the west side of the building was damaged, but remained standing. The masonry facade did not continue to the ground, but was supported on a steel angle at the level of the second-story floor. On the west side of the building, this wall was crushed at the toe (fig. 3.50). On the east side of the building, the entire wall came off the supporting angle. The connections between the wall and the building frame appeared to be minimal (fig. 3.51). Other than these end walls, the building performed well. In the longitudinal direction, only a few panes of glass were broken on the first story.

A steel-frame office building on the west side of Topanga Canyon Boulevard in Canoga Park, housing the American Savings Bank, experienced significant movement in its first story columns, apparently swaying in a north-south direction during the quake. It did not return to its original position, but suffered a permanent offset to the north (fig. 3.52). A nearly identical building on the same site, oriented at right angles to the first, had only minor damage to glass at the first story. The first-story column heights of the two building differed significantly: the columns in the undamaged building were noticeably shorter than the columns in the damaged structure. The damaged building illustrates the classic problem of a "soft" first story. It is interesting to note that several glass-clad high-rise buildings in the vicinity showed no evidence of damage.

The business district along Ventura Boulevard in Sherman Oaks was another area with significant numbers of badly damaged buildings. The 13-story Trans World Bank Building is located at 15233 Ventura Boulevard (fig. 3.53). There is a two-level underground garage below the building and a mechanical penthouse on the roof. This reinforced concrete frame building was designed under the 1964 Los Angeles City code. Structural damage was in the first-story columns, primarily at the second-floor beam-column joints. Identical failures occurred during the 1971 San Fernando earthquake. The damaged joints were repaired with epoxy shortly after the 1994 earthquake (fig. 3.54).

The Radisson Valley Center Hotel is located at 15433 Ventura Boulevard in Sherman Oaks (fig. 3.55). This 13-story concrete structure sustained serious damage to columns located at the first and fifth stories. Exterior columns which support the three-story appendage at the front of the hotel were also damaged (fig. 3.56)

The 22-story American Pacific State Bank is located diagonally across from the damaged Radisson Hotel (fig. 3.57). The building is clad with large glass windows, and there was no evidence of window or other damage. However, the eight-story parking garage behind the bank sustained damage to columns. They were being repaired shortly after the quake.

A four-story steel frame structure located at the intersection of Moorpark Street and Cedros Avenue in Sherman Oaks was shaken seriously during the earthquake (fig. 3.58). The exterior reinforced masonry wall was cracked in many places, particularly at the second floor level (fig. 3.59). The evidence of large ground shaking in the Sherman Oaks area was also seen by serious lateral displacements of single family houses and three-story apartment buildings from their foundation. In fact, a strong-motion instrument station in Tarzana located only a few kilometers away from this general area recorded the largest acceleration in this earthquake (1.82g horizontal, 1.18g vertical).

In the weeks following the quake, reports surfaced about surprisingly large numbers of damaged steel-frame buildings, which, as a class, have been considered relatively earthquake-resistant. Failure modes reported include brittle fractures of column flanges, base plates, and welds at connections; and buckling of diagonal tube bracing (Los Angeles Times, Feb. 27, 1994) [2]. The team did not observe any of this damage, which is ordinarily concealed behind fireproofing and finish materials. Further documentation of failures in steel frame buildings is needed.

Figure 3.41.   The second story of the concrete frame Kaiser Permanente office building on Balboa Avenue in Granada Hills completely collapsed. The first story was relatively undamaged, suggesting it was far stiffer than the story above.

Figure 3.42.   Both end walls of the Kaiser Permanente building slid, partially intact, to the ground. The south wall is pictured here. Both ends of the building suffered damage to the concrete frame at all story levels, while the middle half of the building, except for the second story, remained intact.

Figure 3.43. Damage at the north end of the building was similar to damage at the south.

Figure 3.44. The exposed concrete frame of the Kaiser Permanente building, revealing deep beams, suggests that the building had a strong-beam, weak-column configuration. Except for the second story columns, the columns and beams remained intact while the joints disintegrated.

Figure 3.45. The six-story L-shaped concrete-frame Barrington Building on Olympic Boulevard in West Los Angeles lost its vertical-load carrying capacity at the second story.

Figure 3.46. The stiff infill panels of the Barrington Building effectively shortened the concrete columns, forcing all the displacement into the column sections bounded by windows. Diagonal X-cracking decreased in severity towards the top of the building.

Figure 3.47. The cracking in the concrete columns at the second story was so extensive that the vertical-load carrying capacity of the building was affected. The building settled 50-100 mm at the second story, as these bulging window frames attest. The worst damage was at the southeast corner, the outside corner of the L-shape, pictured here. The building, which developed a slight list, was demolished within days of the quake.

Figure 3.48. A close up of the damaged southeast corner of the Barrington Building shows the widely spaced, undeformed bars used for transverse reinforcement.

Figure 3.49. The east end wall and stair tower of a five-story apparently steel-framed office building on Sherman Way in Reseda collapsed. The enclosing masonry wall became detached from the structure and slid to the ground, with the upper stories remaining intact. The doorway opening in the wall, shown here resting at about the second story level, originally provided access from the top story to the stair tower.

Figure 3.50. The similar west wall of was damaged, but did not peel away from the structure. This close up of the interface between the first and second stories shows that the masonry facade is supported on a steel angle. At the west end of the building, the facade was crushed at the toe where it is supported by the angle.

Figure 3.51. The exposed structure of the Sherman Way office building shows remains (at the floor level and the column) of the minimal ties that anchored the masonry facade.

Figure 3.52. The first-story columns of the steel-framed building housing the American Savings Bank on Topanga Canyon Road in Canoga Park flexed during the quake and ended up slightly displaced from their original positions.

Figure 3.53. The Trans World Bank building, in Sherman Oaks, was damaged in both the 1971 San Fernando and 1994 Northridge earthquakes.

Figure 3.54. The cracked beam-column joints between the first and second stories of the Trans World Bank building were repaired using epoxy injection.

Figure 3.55. The concrete Radisson Valley Center Hotel in Sherman Oaks had serious damage to the columns at the first and fifth stories.

Figure 3.56. The columns supporting the three-story appendage at the front of the Radisson Hotel had serious shear cracks and related spalling.

Figure 3.57. There was no evidence of damage to the 22-story American Pacific State Bank in Sherman Oaks. The adjacent eight-story parking garage had damaged columns.

Figure 3.58. The reinforced masonry facade of this steel-framed building in Sherman Oaks was badly damaged.

Figure 3.59.   A close-up view of the damage shows the pattern of reinforcing used in the masonry facade.

3.4 Parking Structures

Eight major public parking structures suffered collapse or severe damage: two at the Northridge Fashion Center, and one each at California State University at Northridge, Sherman Oaks Fashion Square, Glendale Fashion Center, Glendale Civic Center, the Trans World Bank in Sherman Oaks, and the Kaiser Permanente West Los Angeles Medical Center (Los Angeles Times, February 4, 1994). Many other parking structures suffered less spectacular, but nevertheless serious, damage. The damaged parking structures were scattered throughout the affected area.

The four-level parking garage at the California State University at Northridge campus was built in 1991 of precast concrete with cast-in-place concrete slabs. The lateral resisting system was an exterior perimeter frame constructed of precast "trees" (columns with half-length beams cast as one piece) connected in the field to form a moment frame. Major portions of the structure collapsed.

The collapse apparently started at the interior of the building. The exterior perimeter frame was pulled over towards the center of the structure (fig. 3.60), suggesting that interior beams had lost their vertical support, causing the floor plates to collapse and pull the exterior walls in with them. While some interior columns had collapsed, others were left intact, jutting up above the fallen floor slabs (fig. 3.61).

The five-level parking garage at the Kaiser Permanente medical complex on Cadillac Avenue in West Los Angeles experienced a similar collapse. All four facades were pulled inward, suggesting that an interior failure precipitated the damage (fig. 3.62). This garage was a post-tensioned cast-in-place concrete structure with shear walls providing the lateral-force resisting system at the east and west ends, and moment frames at the north and south perimeter. The shear walls were cracked horizontally throughout their height due to the out-of-plane bending (fig. 3.63). There was minor diagonal cracking, suggesting that the lateral load was not fully transmitted to the shear walls. The stair towers remained standing. Typically, these towers are structurally isolated from the post-tensioned slab to minimize potential deformations in the towers due to creep and shrinkage in the post-tensioned slabs.

The two-level concrete parking structure adjacent to the Trans World Bank in Sherman Oaks had been seismically strengthened after suffering serious damage in the 1971 San Fernando quake. Flared extensions were cast next to the interior columns along their north-south axes (fig. 3.64), creating short wing walls supporting the precast beams. During the 1994 quake, the unrehabilitated exterior columns were badly cracked (fig. 3.65). The ramp was also heavily damaged. The interior columns were relatively undamaged.

At the Northridge Fashion Center, three parking structures suffered damage. A large three-level concrete garage at the south end of the site, approximately 10 years old, suffered an almost complete collapse. The largely pre-cast concrete structure had intermittent shear walls which remained standing (fig. 3.66). The lack of diagonal cracks in these walls suggests that, like the walls at the Kaiser Permanente garage, they were never fully loaded. A similar, but smaller, precast garage at the north end of the Northridge Fashion Center also partially collapsed (fig. 3.68). At the east end of the site, an older two-level cast-in-place concrete garage showed evidence of movement. All visible columns had spalled at the top, implying that the beams and slab had interacted in a weak-column/strong-beam frame action.

Common types of damage in other parking garages included shear-failure in unintentional short columns created by ramps or split-level decks (fig. 3.67) and collapsed decks caused by inverted-T's or concrete planks pulling off supports (fig. 3.68).

Much of the damage in parking structures was due to configuration problems inherent in garages: there are minimal amounts of nonstructural elements such as walls and facade that add stiffness and energy-absorbing capacity in other types of buildings; configuration requirements can lead to lack of redundancy in the structural systems; long spans are common; inclined ramps cause incomplete diaphragms and short columns; topping can create an artificially thick slab which may lead to weak-column/strong beam action. Precast concrete also has inherent seismic problems: precast buildings are typically massive and thus generate high inertial forces; it is difficult to provide ductility in the joints; because it is necessary to allow for movement due to shrinkage, creep, thermal changes, etc., it can be difficult to ensure a complete load-path. When garages are constructed of precast concrete members, special care must be taken to address all these potential problems.

Figure 3.60.   The three-year old four-level parking garage at the Northridge campus of California State University partially collapsed in the earthquake. The collapse apparently started at the interior, causing the exterior frame to be pulled in to the middle of the structure. Precast concrete "trees" were connected to form a moment-resisting frame at the exterior of the structure.

Figure 3.61.   Some interior columns of the Northridge campus parking garage remained standing.

Figure 3.62. The cast-in-place concrete parking garage at the Kaiser Permanente Hospital complex in West Los Angeles collapsed in on itself. The moment frame that provided lateral resistance on the south face of the structure could not resist the out-of-plane forces apparently caused by the collapse of interior elements.

Figure 3.63. At the east and west faces of the Kaiser Permanente Hospital parking garage, shear walls made up the lateral force resisting system. Both walls had horizontal cracks caused by the out-of-plane bending when the walls were pulled inward. Neither wall had major diagonal cracking, suggesting that the lateral load was never fully delivered to the walls. The stair towers remained erect. The east wall and stair tower are shown here.

Figure 3.64. The interior columns of the two-level parking garage at the Trans World Bank in Sherman Oaks had been seismically strengthened after it suffered damage in the 1971 San Fernando quake. The interior columns fared well in the 1994 Northridge quake.

Figure 3.65. The exterior columns of the Trans World Bank parking garage, which had not been strengthened, were badly damaged.

Figure 3.66. At the Northridge Fashion Center, major portions of the three-level south parking garage collapsed. The garage was precast concrete with intermittent shear walls. Most of the shear walls remained standing, largely undamaged, indicating that the lateral load was not adequately transmitted to these walls.

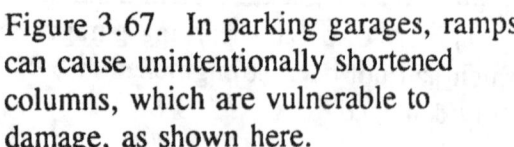

Figure 3.67. In parking garages, ramps can cause unintentionally shortened columns, which are vulnerable to damage, as shown here.

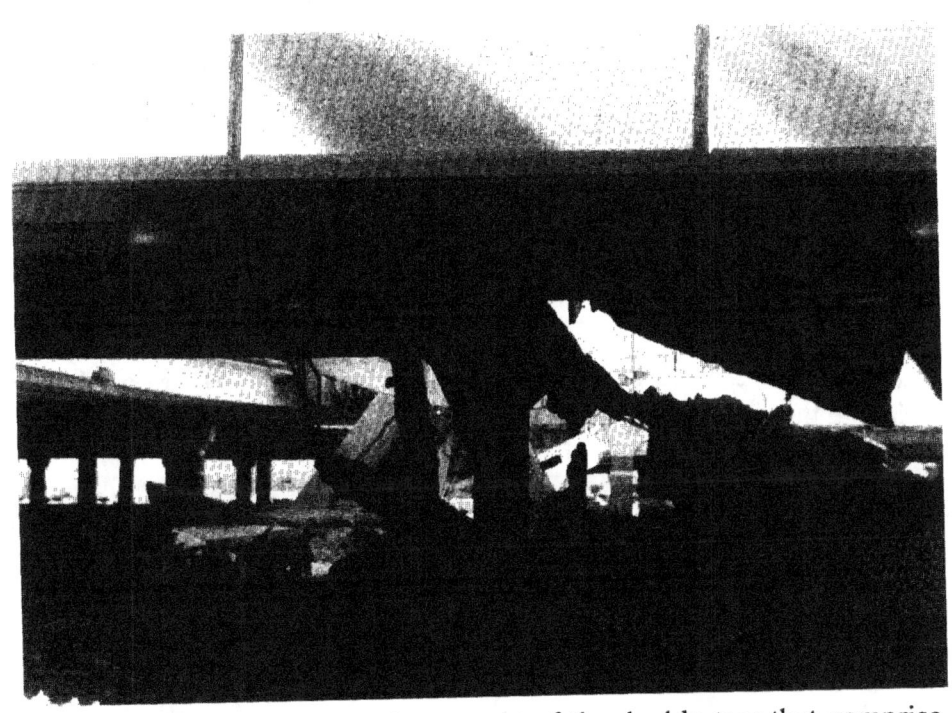

Figure 3.68.   In precast parking garages, the support of the double-tees that comprise the
floors is a vulnerable link in the system. This garage, at the north end of the
Northridge Fashion Center, illustrates a common failure: the double-tees
pulled off their supports, leaving the supporting elements essentially intact.

3.5 Comparison with Effects of the 1971 San Fernando Quake

In 1971, the San Fernando Valley was devastated by a magnitude 6.6 quake centered in Sylmar, about 25 km northeast of the Northridge epicenter. These two quakes provide a unique opportunity for us to examine how well the U.S. earthquake engineering community learned the lessons of the 1971 quake.

Some of the findings and recommendations published after the 1971 event sound almost identical to those heard in the days and weeks following the Northridge event.

"Numerous recordings of horizontal accelerations which greatly exceeded those envisioned in formulating the current lateral force requirements are reason to review and possibly increase seismic coefficients currently in use." [15]

"In view of records of vertical ground accelerations of the same order of magnitude as horizontal accelerations, the presence of vertical seismic forces can no longer be ignored." [15]

"Deformation and deflection, as well as strength, should be considered in earthquake-resistant design." [15]

"Numerous failures were observed in apartments and single-family homes where large openings in walls were provided for garages or entranceways." [15]

"Comfort must not be sought in the fact that there was only minimal structural damage to the new buildings because, in some instances, these same buildings suffered considerable nonstructural damage which could have been an extreme hazard to its occupants." [15]

"Improved methods for supporting mobile homes should be developed and implemented." [15]

However, the fact that each of these observations and recommendations could be made again today in light of the Northridge earthquake does not mean that no progress has been made in the intervening years. In fact, the Northridge earthquake demonstrated some dramatic improvements in seismic hazard mitigation practices for buildings.

Hospitals fared dramatically better in 1994. In 1971, three hospital complexes, the Olive View Medical Center, the San Fernando Veterans Administration Hospital, and the Holy Cross Hospital, suffered major structural damage, leading to collapse or demolition of some buildings. Several other hospital complexes had serious structural damage but no complete collapses. In 1994, structural damage in hospitals built after 1971 was almost non-existent.

In 1971, a significant number of single family houses collapsed, particularly split-level houses [15]. Relatively few single family houses collapsed in 1994.

As a class, unreinforced masonry buildings performed poorly in 1971. There were two complete collapses of pre-1933 masonry buildings on the grounds of the Olive View Hospital complex

[16]. Another masonry building on site was so badly damaged it was later pulled down. Portions of masonry walls were dislodged as far as 30 km away, in central Los Angeles. Because the 1971 quake was centered in the northern section of the San Fernando Valley, areas such as Santa Monica and Hollywood, which have large concentrations of unreinforced masonry buildings, were not severely shaken. One contemporary report speculated, "It is clear that if the earthquake had centered some 20 miles farther south, in the old part of town, many old buildings would have collapsed." [16] The 1994 event did occur about that distance to the south, but the predicted collapses did not occur. This must be attributed, at least in part, to the fact that a significant portion of the vulnerable unreinforced masonry buildings in the area had been seismically rehabilitated prior to the quake.

3.6 Summary

The strong shaking of the 1994 magnitude 6.8 Northridge earthquake challenged the lateral force resisting systems of the buildings in the San Fernando Valley area. The vast majority of affected buildings successfully met the challenge, retaining their structural integrity, even though non-structural elements and contents were damaged. From the behavior of the buildings that did not perform successfully, the following conclusions can be drawn:

- In most cases, buildings designed and constructed using modern (mid-1970's or later) seismic requirements performed well structurally. Most buildings that did collapse either:
  - had a structural system known to be vulnerable to earthquake damage, such as unreinforced masonry walls or non-ductile concrete frames, or
  - were sited in a situation known to be vulnerable, such as on or below a steep hillside.

  Structural damage that was not due to one of these causes included fractures in steel frame buildings (which have traditionally been considered inherently earthquake-resistant) and damage to parking garages.

- Many lessons learned from previous earthquakes were demonstrated again in the Northridge quake:
  - a complete load path is necessary to transmit the earthquake-induced forces to the elements designed to resist them
  - nonstructural damage can cause hospitals, schools, businesses, and industrial facilities to be inoperable, even if structural damage is slight or non-existent
  - manufactured homes will be severely damaged or destroyed if they are not adequately anchored

- Soft first stories due to open parking space with few walls below stiffer upper stories are vulnerable to excessive distortion and collapse.

- Structural elements that are not considered a part of the lateral-force-resisting system can fail and initiate collapse if they are not detailed to accommodate drift.

- The unique configuration problems of parking garages (ramps, short columns, incomplete diaphragms) suggest that they need special design consideration.

- Rehabilitation of unreinforced masonry buildings using bolts to connect horizontal diaphragms to walls provides only limited improvement - most total collapses were avoided, but serious cracking of masonry and some loss of brick was nevertheless widespread.

3.7 Suggestions for Improving Practice

From common aspects of the buildings that were damaged, suggestions for improving seismic mitigation practices for buildings can be developed.

1. Involve the community in decisions on the level of performance to be required in the building codes.

Our country's building codes are intended to protect life-safety but not to limit economic losses. Greater levels of earthquake protection can be provided. In general, our understanding of earthquake motions and building responses is sufficient to allow buildings to be designed and constructed to be functional after a design-level quake. However, this added protection adds to the cost of design and construction. The question of how much protection to provide is not one for engineers to answer alone. All affected parts of society should participate in the weighing of costs against benefits to determine how much protection of property and function should be required by building codes.

2. Educate code users to improve the quality of new buildings.

Many failures occurred at locations of abrupt changes in the strength or stiffness of a building: the failed second story of the Kaiser Permanente building on Balboa Avenue; the sheared columns stiffened by infill at Champagne Towers and the Barrington Building; the offset first story columns in the steel-frame building housing the American Savings Bank on Topanga Canyon Boulevard. These failures emphasize the need for buildings to be designed as integral, interactive systems rather than mere agglomerations of code-complying parts. Successful designs will consider the behavior of the entire structure under earthquake loads.

Another significant category of failures resulted from incomplete or inadequate load paths. Shear walls of the Northridge Fashion Center parking garage were left standing, uncracked, when the columns and slabs around them fell, indicating that the lateral load was never transferred to these elements that were intended to resist them. The office building on Sherman Way with inadequate connections between the masonry facade on the transverse end wall and the structure is another example of costly damage caused by an incomplete load path.

Overall building behavior and complete load paths are not design aspects that lend themselves to codification. No building code can anticipate every possible building design and be written to prevent any possible problem. Insightful use of the code by the designers is required. Significant improvements in the seismic capacity of our nation's building stock requires education of building designers and constructors to impart an understanding of building behavior in earthquakes, and how their efforts can affect that behavior. This earthquake has demonstrated that the building codes in force in the affected area are very effective when they are insightfully applied. Education of practicing architects, engineers, contractors, and building officials through seminars, videos, pamphlets, and other methods, and education of future designers and builders through universities and trade schools is recommended. Development and wide, low-cost distribution of design guides for architects and engineers is also suggested.

3. Actively reduce the worst risks in existing buildings.

This earthquake demonstrated once again the imperative need to address the problem of improving the seismic safety of existing buildings that are known to be vulnerable, particularly unreinforced masonry and non-ductile concrete frame buildings.

A re-evaluation of the effectiveness and cost of rehabilitation of unreinforced masonry buildings should be undertaken. Comprehensive studies of the performance of all unreinforced masonry buildings in the affected area, both rehabilitated and unrehabilitated, should be performed to determine, statistically rather than anecdotally, the efficacy of various strengthening techniques. This earthquake showed that the application of the current rehabilitation requirements does not prevent life-threatening damage from occurring, but it does seem to prevent total collapse. The cost and relative effectiveness of more drastic measures for minimizing falling brick, such as covering the masonry with a layer of shotcrete, should be investigated.

The impact of a mandated rehabilitation requirement for high-occupancy non-ductile concrete frame buildings should be studied. The Bullock's department store and Kaiser Permanente office building collapses demonstrated the potential for large loss of life that these buildings pose.

4. Develop improved requirements and design guidelines for specific building types and systems.

Improved design guidance should be developed for nonstructural systems, with particular attention given to performance requirements of essential facilities.

The behavior of parking garages should be compared to the behavior of comparable buildings (similar lateral force resisting systems, natural periods, level of ground shaking) to ascertain the effect of interior partitions, exterior finishes, and other building-specific characteristics on seismic performance. If found appropriate, special design provisions for parking structures should be developed.

CHAPTER 4

PERFORMANCE OF BRIDGES

4.1 Overview

The vast majority of bridges in the Los Angeles metropolitan area performed well in the Northridge earthquake. Nonetheless, there were several cases of severe damage to bridges, or bridge collapses, which seriously impacted transportation patterns in the Los Angeles metropolitan area. Besides the direct cost of repairing or replacing earthquake damaged bridges, there were tremendous economic and social costs resulting from transportation delays. In addition, bridges which were taken out of service by the earthquake hampered emergency response efforts immediately after the event.

According to statistics compiled by Willman et al. [17], there are approximately 12 000 state-owned highway bridges in California, and 2523 of these are located in Los Angeles County. In California, 1313 highway bridges have been identified by the California Department of Transportation (Caltrans) as needing seismic retrofitting, and of these about 20 percent have been retrofitted. Of the highway bridges in Los Angeles County, 716 need seismic retrofitting, and about 16 percent of these have been retrofitted.

Before 1971 the total cost of seismic damage to highway bridges in California was about $100,000. In the 1971 San Fernando earthquake, the cost of damage to highway bridges totaled about $15 million. In the Northridge earthquake, six major highway bridges collapsed, and 157 other highway bridges were damaged. The estimated cost to replace or repair these bridges is $1.5 billion. Before the Northridge earthquake, the estimated cost of retrofitting the approximately 1000 bridges remaining on the Caltrans retrofit list was $1.1 billion.

In addition to the 2523 highway bridges in Los Angeles County, there are about 1500 street bridges owned by the Los Angeles County Government, and 800 street bridges owned by the City of Los Angeles. Before the Northridge earthquake it was estimated that between one-fourth and one-third of these bridges required seismic retrofitting, at a cost of approximately $250 million.

County and City bridges suffered less damage than Interstate and State highway bridges in the Northridge earthquake. Only four of the bridges owned by Los Angeles County suffered significant damage. The total cost of earthquake damage to County bridges is estimated at $1.6 million. Two City bridges (one a pedestrian overcrossing) were closed because of earthquake damage, and another 60 suffered minor damage. The total cost of damage to City bridges was estimated at $2 million. Since 1990, the City of Los Angeles has spent $12.9 million for retrofitting bridges, and altogether $97 million will be spent by 1996 to retrofit 187 City bridges.

In this chapter an overview is presented of the evolution of seismic design and retrofit provisions for bridges in California. This is followed by descritpions of damage to bridges observed following the Northridge earthquake. Finally, conclusions are drawn and recommendations are made for future action to improve the seismic performance of bridges.

4.2 Review of Caltrans Seismic Design and Retrofit Program

4.2.1 Chronology of Seismic Design Criteria Adoption

Until relatively recently, almost all consideration of earthquake forces on structures and relevant code provisions have been concentrated in building construction. The first requirement in the United States for inclusion of seismic loading in the design of highway bridges was that of the California State Highway Department in 1940 and the American Association of State Highway Officials (AASHO)[1] in 1941.

The first edition of the Standard Specifications for Highway Bridges was issued by the American AASHO in 1931. Since that time, the Federal Highway Administration (FHWA) and its predecessor, the Bureau of Public Roads (BPR), have required that bridges constructed with Federal funds be designed in accordance with these specifications.

Prior to 1941, AASHO bridge design specifications did not mention earthquake loads. However, in 1933, the design calculations and specifications for the San Francisco-Oakland Bay Bridge required that a static force of 7.5 percent of the force of gravity be applied as an earthquake load. The 1940 California State Highway Department (now known as Caltrans) bridge design specifications indicated that the exact earthquake load applied to a structure should be determined by the engineer; a specific value was not defined.

The 1941, 1944, and 1949 editions of the AASHO bridge design specifications in Article 3.2.1- Loads, simply stated that "Structures shall be proportioned for . . . earthquake stresses." Article 3.4.1 of the specifications stated that structures designed for loads in combination with an earthquake load be designed for allowable stresses increased by 25 percent. However, there was no recommendation or criterion as to how the earthquake load was to be determined or how it was to be applied to the structure.

Several revisions to the Caltrans and AASHO seismic design criteria were made between 1940 and 1971. The revisions were based on the same concept as the earlier criteria, namely the application of a specified static lateral force to the structure.

The San Fernando earthquake of 1971 generated a revolution in earthquake design criteria. Immediate changes were instituted by Caltrans to increase the 1963 code earthquake load level by a factor of at least 2 for all bridges. In addition to the increased earthquake load level, structural details were toughened considerably, and a seismic retrofit program was instituted.

In 1972, the FHWA encouraged the use of the 1963 California formulation for lateral seismic design force with the addition of a seismic risk zone coefficient for a more general application throughout the country. The FHWA considered this formulation as an interim measure until the AASHTO Specifications could be revised.

---

[1] AASHO is the predecessor of AASHTO, the American Association of State Highway and Transportation Officials.

In 1973, a major revision in seismic design criteria was instituted by Caltrans. It was initially introduced in the form of a design memorandum, and was formally published as Design Specifications in 1974. This utilized a maximum credible earthquake map developed by the California Division of Mines and Geology to define earthquake potential in the State. It also introduced the design of restraining features to limit the relative displacements of the superstructure.

The 1975 AASHTO Interim Specifications were expanded to include the earthquake criteria developed by Caltrans in 1973. A seismic risk map of the United States was included in this edition.

In 1983 after substantial Caltrans- and FHWA-sponsored research, an AASHTO Guide Specifications for Seismic Design of Highway Bridges was published. The 1983 AASHTO Standard Specifications for Highway Bridges, retained the requirements of the 1975 AASHTO Interim Specifications, but allowed the designer the option of using the Guide Specification.

The 1989 AASHTO Standard Specifications stated:

In regions where earthquakes may be anticipated, structures shall be designed to resist earthquake motions by considering the relationship of the site to active faults, the seismic response of the soils at the site, and the dynamic response characteristics of the total structure in accordance with the following criteria or AASHTO Guide Specifications of Seismic Design of Highway Bridges.

The criteria in the 1989 Standard Specifications generally were based on the 1973 Earthquake Design Criteria for Bridges issued by the State of California. The California criteria were developed for California conditions and subsequently modified to allow for their use in other areas of the United States. The 1983 AASHTO guide specification was incorporated in the standard specification in 1992, three years after the Loma Prieta earthquake.

The Caltrans design criteria have been revised periodically since 1974. The most recent update was in 1989 with the refinement of its ARS elastic response spectra, where A, R, and S are factors related to the maximum expected bedrock acceleration, a normalized rock response, and a soil amplification spectral ratio. The Caltrans approach reduces the elastic response spectra to strength design spectra through an adjustment factor, Z, to account for ductility and risk as a function of structure period, type, and component. Both the Caltrans and AASHTO design approaches continue to be evaluated and refined.

4.2.2 Seismic Retrofitting of Bridges

The primary goal of seismic retrofitting is to minimize the risk of unacceptable damage during the design earthquake. Damage is unacceptable if it results in the collapse of all or part of the bridge or the loss of use of a vital transportation route which may pass over or under the bridge.

Seismic retrofitting of existing highway bridges is a relatively new concept in bridge engineering. It was motivated by the damage sustained by highway bridges during the 1971 San Fernando earthquake. The 1971 earthquake clearly pointed out the existence of a number of deficiencies in the then current bridge design specifications. It also focused on the fact that numerous existing bridges may be expected to fail in some major way during their remaining life if subjected to strong ground shaking.

Following the poor performance of several bridges in the San Fernando earthquake, Caltrans, FHWA, and subsequently other State highway agencies began studies into the seismic performance of bridges. This effort resulted in a series of publications, interim specifications, and seismic design guidelines for both new and existing bridges.

One such effort resulted in a report entitled "Seismic Retrofitting Guidelines for Highway Bridges," in 1983 [18]. The report illustrates retrofit concepts that can be applied to existing bridges to enhance the probability of their survival when subjected to postulated seismic motions. In 1994, a report entitled "Seismic Retrofitting Manual for Highway Bridges," (1994) [19], was published to reflect the development of technology during the previous ten years. The manual offers procedures for evaluating and upgrading the seismic resistance of existing bridges. It does not prescribe rigid requirements for when and how bridges are to be retrofitted. The decision to retrofit a bridge depends on a number of factors, several of which are outside the realm of engineering, such as the availability of funding as well as political, social, and economic considerations. The manual assists in evaluating the engineering factors.

Because of the difficulty and cost involved in strengthening an existing bridge to comply with new design standards, it is usually not economically justifiable to do so. For this reason, the goal of retrofitting is limited to preventing collapse while permitting structural damage during a major earthquake. In some cases, the ability of the bridge to carry light emergency traffic immediately following an earthquake is also important. The threshold of damage that constitutes unacceptable failure must be defined by the engineer by considering the overall configuration of the structure, the importance of the structure as a lifeline following a major earthquake, the ease with which certain types of damage can be repaired quickly, and the relationship of the bridge to other structures that may be affected during the same earthquake. Because of the complexity of these decisions and the many non-engineering factors involved, a considerable amount of judgement is required.

The Caltrans seismic retrofit program began in 1971 after the San Fernando earthquake. The heaviest concentration of highway damage caused by the 1971 earthquake occurred in the vicinity of I5 and I210. Portions of I5, I405, State Routes 2 and 14 also sustained moderate to heavy damage. Five freeway overpasses collapsed.

The San Fernando earthquake prompted Caltrans to examine and extensively revise its seismic design criteria, and to embark on a seismic retrofit program for its vulnerable structures. The retrofit program began with three phases:

Phase I - Superstructure joint and hinge restrainers, shear keys and vertical restrainers.

Phase II - Single column bents.

Phase III - Multi-column bents.

Phase I consisted of tying bridge spans together at joints and hinges with longitudinal steel cables or rod restrainers. This program also included installation of horizontal shear keys at many superstructure joints to prevent lateral translation of the spans. Vertical restrainers were also installed on some structures. In addition to the normal restrainer devices, innovative devices were developed to solve unusual problems. Massive truss and steel girder bridges on tall columns with narrow seats required larger restrainers than ordinarily used.

Phase I addressed what Caltrans considered to be the most critical bridge deficiency: the potential loss of bearing support for girders. The goal of the program was to prevent bridge collapse and allow passage of emergency vehicles. The possibility of significant damage to some structures was not precluded. The retrofit philosophy was to minimize differential movements, mobilize the damping effects of columns, and restrict longitudinal movement to existing bearing seat widths.

Phase I took about 17 years to accomplish at a very low funding level of $3 to $4 million per year. Approximately 1500 bridges were retrofitted under this program at a total cost of about $55 million. Phase I was nearly complete when the Whittier earthquake struck the Los Angeles area on October 1, 1987. The only bridge which sustained major damage was the I605 overpass structure of the I5/I605 interchange. The interchange was immediately closed, but was reopened within 24 hours after Caltrans installed temporary falsework. The substructure on this bridge, which consisted of five-column bents, suffered shear failure. Columns were severely cracked and spalled. Cracking in the bent caps also occurred adjacent to the columns, probably as a the result of plastic hinging in this area. Nine other bridges on various routes suffered minor damage to bearing seats, wingwalls, bridge rails, joints, and curtain walls.

The Whittier earthquake was the first major test of the Caltrans retrofit program. In the area which experienced high intensity earthquake motion, 75 bridges were identified as vulnerable to collapse. These bridges had been retrofitted with restrainers at a cost of about $3 million. The replacement cost for these bridges at that time was estimated to be $98 million. The retrofit cost was a modest amount compared with the replacement cost for these structures. The successful performance of the restrainers during the Whittier earthquake seemed to confirm retrofit design and program priorities of Caltrans.

However, on October 17, 1989, the devastating magnitude 7.1 Loma Prieta earthquake struck Northern California. Strong shaking lasted only 10 to 15 seconds but resulted in the death of 62 people and injuries to more than 3 000 others. More than 12 000 people were displaced from their homes and total property damage was over $6 billion [7].

The greatest tragedies, which accounted for two-thirds of the total deaths, were the collapse of major sections of the I880 Cypress Viaduct in Oakland where 42 people died, and the collapse of a span of the San Francisco-Oakland Bay Bridge which resulted in two deaths. One other bridge, the Struve Slough bridge near Watsonville, also collapsed, but fortunately the collapse did not result in any deaths.

The Loma Prieta earthquake was the largest on the San Andreas fault since the great San Francisco earthquake of 1906. The epicenter of the Loma Prieta earthquake was approximately 100 km south-southeast of San Francisco and 15 km northeast of Santa Cruz. The earthquake was felt from Los Angeles to the south, Oregon to the north, and western Nevada to the east. The disaster caused a critical reexamination of seismic needs for State and local bridges and resulted in a significant increase in State and Federal funding for seismic research and retrofitting. Annual funding for seismic research increased from approximately $500 000 to $5 million and seismic retrofitting technology has advanced significantly in the past four years.

With the increased funding, Caltrans accelerated its seismic retrofit program which was reorganized into a new Phase 2 to replace the old Phases II and III. Phase 2 will address single-column bents, double-deck viaducts, multi-column bents and other complex bridges. All bridges will be evaluated to determine their seismic vulnerability and retrofit priorities.

The current seismic retrofit philosophy of Caltrans is to increase the seismic resistance of a bridge to the point of preventing collapse and thereby avoiding loss of life [20]. Bridges which are identified as "important" will receive a higher level of retrofit so that they can remain serviceable following a major (maximum credible) earthquake.

The design procedure for seismic retrofitting of bridges in California [20] has gained sophistication over the past several years. Current analysis and design methods focus on several key items which are fundamental to ensuring the desired performance of a retrofitted structure under seismic loads. These include understanding global structural behavior, displacement or curvature ductility, beam-column joint performance, hinge and restrainer behavior, and foundation interactions.

With approximately 24 000 State and local bridges in its inventory, Caltrans developed a screening process for determining which bridges are the most critical. This screening process considered the following items:

- year of construction
- expected ground acceleration, which takes into account distance from an active fault and soil conditions
- number of columns in the bents
- existing confinement reinforcement in the columns
- length of the structure
- annual daily traffic
- route type
- availability of detour
- structure skew

Of the approximately 12 000 State bridges, about 2500 are supported on single column bents and 9500 on multi-column bents. As of February 1, 1994, the Caltrans screening process and follow-up structural analysis had identified about 259 bridges with single-column bents and 780 bridges with multi-column bents that needed seismic retrofitting [21]. For the 12 000 local bridges, which are generally smaller in size, 173 bridges were initially identified as requiring retrofitting. An additional 1500 local bridges still need evaluation by Caltrans.

Prior to the Northridge earthquake, approximately 120 structures in the Los Angeles area had gone through Phase 2 retrofitting. Most of the projects included the application of steel jackets around single column bents to better confine the core concrete. It is reported that none of the 120 bridges experienced any column damage with the exception of some minor flexural yielding in the area between the top of the steel jacket and the soffit of the column cap beam [22].

The current seismic retrofit program is proceeding at an accelerated pace. The end of 1995 has been identified as a target date for completion of retrofit of State bridges. Evidence indicates that the original Phase I hinge and joint retrofit program was effective in preventing the collapse of numerous bridges during the Whittier, Loma Prieta, and Northridge earthquakes. This gives confidence that the implementation of hinge and joint restraint improvements represents one of the most cost effective retrofit technologies that can be implemented. It does not "earthquake proof" a bridge, but it can reduce the potential for span collapse in moderate seismic events. Caltrans has consistently taken full advantage of lessons learned from past earthquakes to update its seismic design and retrofit procedures.

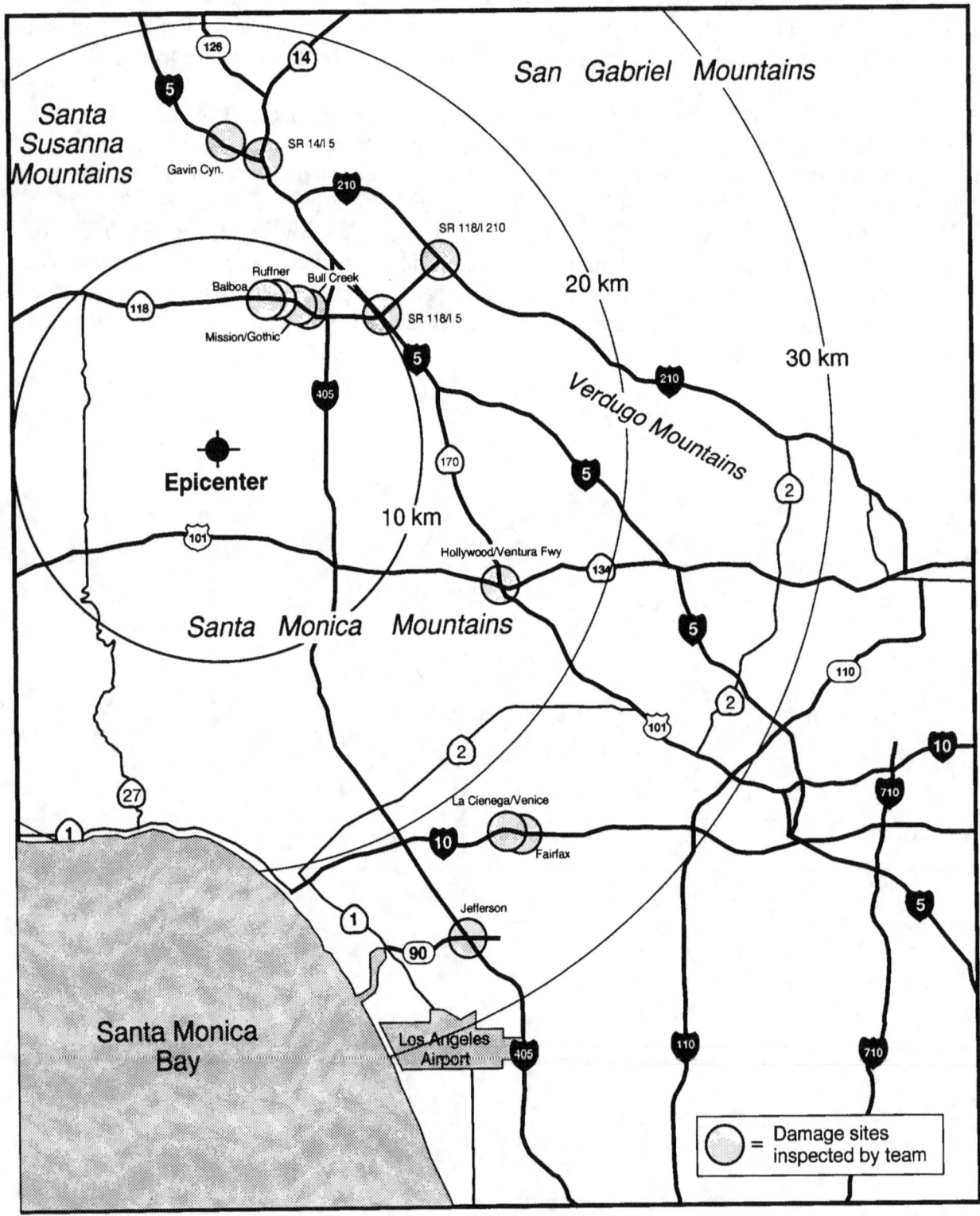

Figure 4.1. Bridge damage sites studied by the reconnaissance team.

4.3 Descriptions of Observed Damage

From January 19 to 23, the reconnaissance team conducted field inspections of highway bridges damaged by the Northridge earthquake. Figure 4.1 shows the locations of the bridges inspected by the reconnaissance team. Because demolition work on collapsed spans was started less than 24 hours after the earthquake, in some cases it was impossible for the reconnaissance team to inspect all of the debris from collapsed spans before it had been disturbed. However, through inspections of the remaining debris, photographs and interviews with other engineers it was possible to reconstruct the pertinent features of the collapses. Below are descriptions of the condition of the most seriously damaged highway bridges.

The assistance of Caltrans in arranging for field inspections and in providing structural drawings and other background information on bridges is gratefully acknowledged. The authors would also like to thank the Earthquake Engineering Research Center (EERC) and the Federal Highway Administration (FHWA) for providing several photographs for this report.

4.3.1 Interstate 5 (the Golden State Freeway) at Gavin Canyon Undercrossing Caltrans bridge number 53-1797

This bridge was designed in 1964 and constructed in 1967. It carries Interstate 5 over Gavin Canyon, about 3 km (2 mi) north of the intersection of Interstate 5 and State Route 14. An aerial photograph of the damaged bridge, after demolition had begun, is shown in figure 4.2, and a ground level view is shown in figure 4.3. Schematic structural drawings are shown in figures 4.4 and 4.5. The structure consists of two parallel bridges, with about a 66 degree skew alignment. Each bridge is composed of five spans. Each bridge has four two-pier bents, and there is a structural hinge near each of the two center bents (figs. 4.3 and 4.4). The superstructure consists of reinforced concrete box girders, and the central portion (between hinges) is post-tensioned. The bridge survived the 1971 San Fernando earthquake with virtually no damage. In 1974, the hinges were retrofitted with cable restrainers, as shown in figure 4.5. The seat length at the hinges is 200 mm (8 in), which by current design standards would be considered inadequate, especially for a structure of this size and flexibility.

Despite the presence of cable restrainers at the hinges, failure of three of the four end spans of the bridge was apparently initiated by the spans falling off the hinge seats. The fourth end span, at the far western corner of the bridge, partially came off its hinge seat but did not collapse, as indicated in figure 4.4. After support was lost at the hinges, a triangular portion of three of the end spans collapsed, as shown in figure 4.4. Demolition of the remaining portions of the end spans was carried out very soon after the earthquake, as shown in figure 4.2. It is likely that the skewed alignment of the bridge was an important contributing factor in this failure. The skewed alignment permitted rotation of the superstructure in a counter-clockwise direction, when viewed from above. The tall, flexible piers of the two center bents would have offered relatively little resistance to rotation in a horizontal plane. (EERC reconnaissance team members noted cracking patterns at the bases of the piers, which may have been evidence of such rotation [5]). Rotation of the superstructure would have resulted in differential displacements at the hinges, and eventually unseating of the end spans at the hinges. Demolition of the bridge was completed a few days after the earthquake.

83

Figure 4.2.   Aerial view of the bridges at Gavin Canyon, looking to the east, showing appearance of the four end spans shortly after demolition had begun.

Figure 4.3.   Ground level view of the southbound bridge at Gavin Canyon, looking to the northwest, showing the hinge bearing seat near Bent 3.

84

I5 GavinCanyon Undercrossing

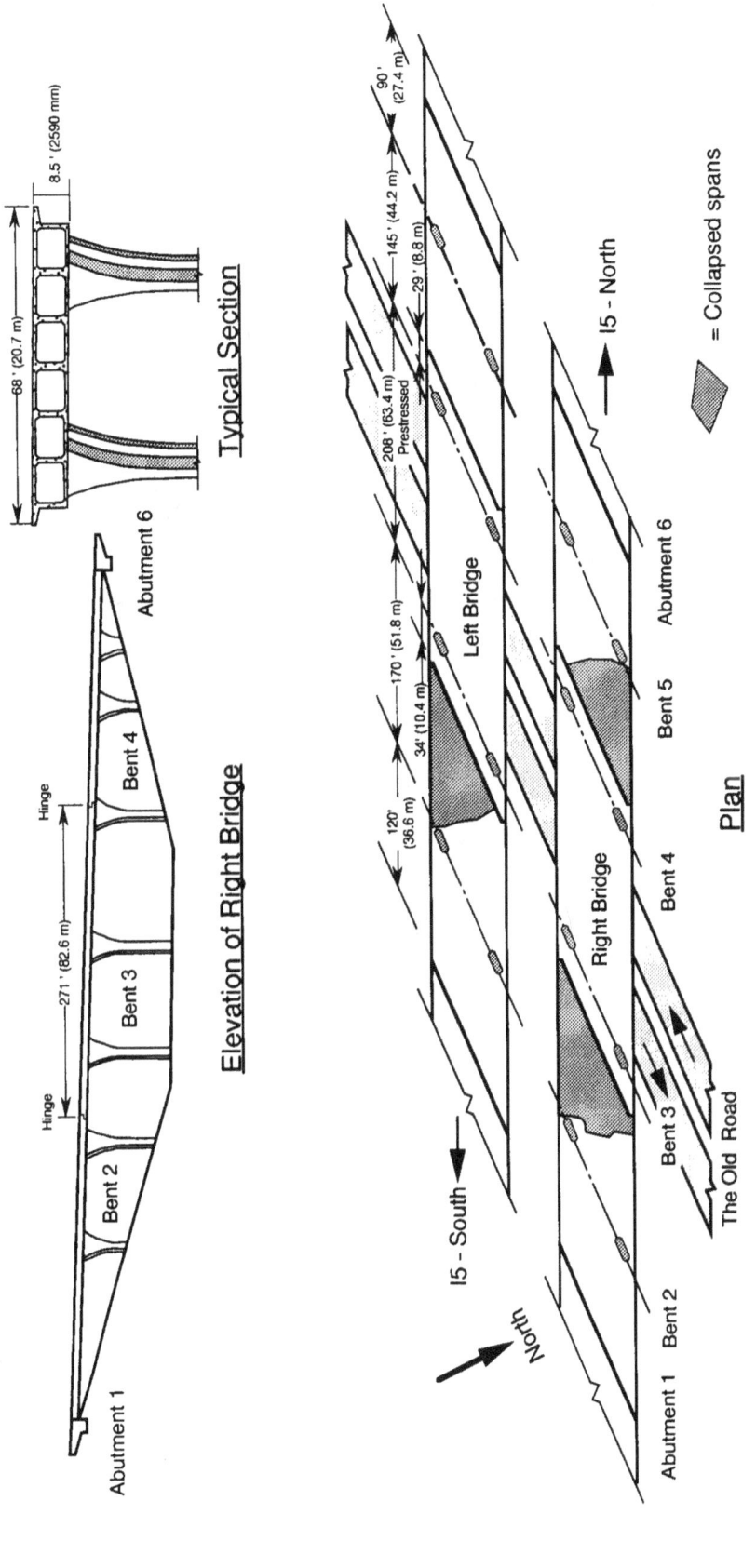

Typical Section

Elevation of Right Bridge

Plan

Figure 4.4. Plan and elevation views of Gavin Canyon Undercrossing.

85

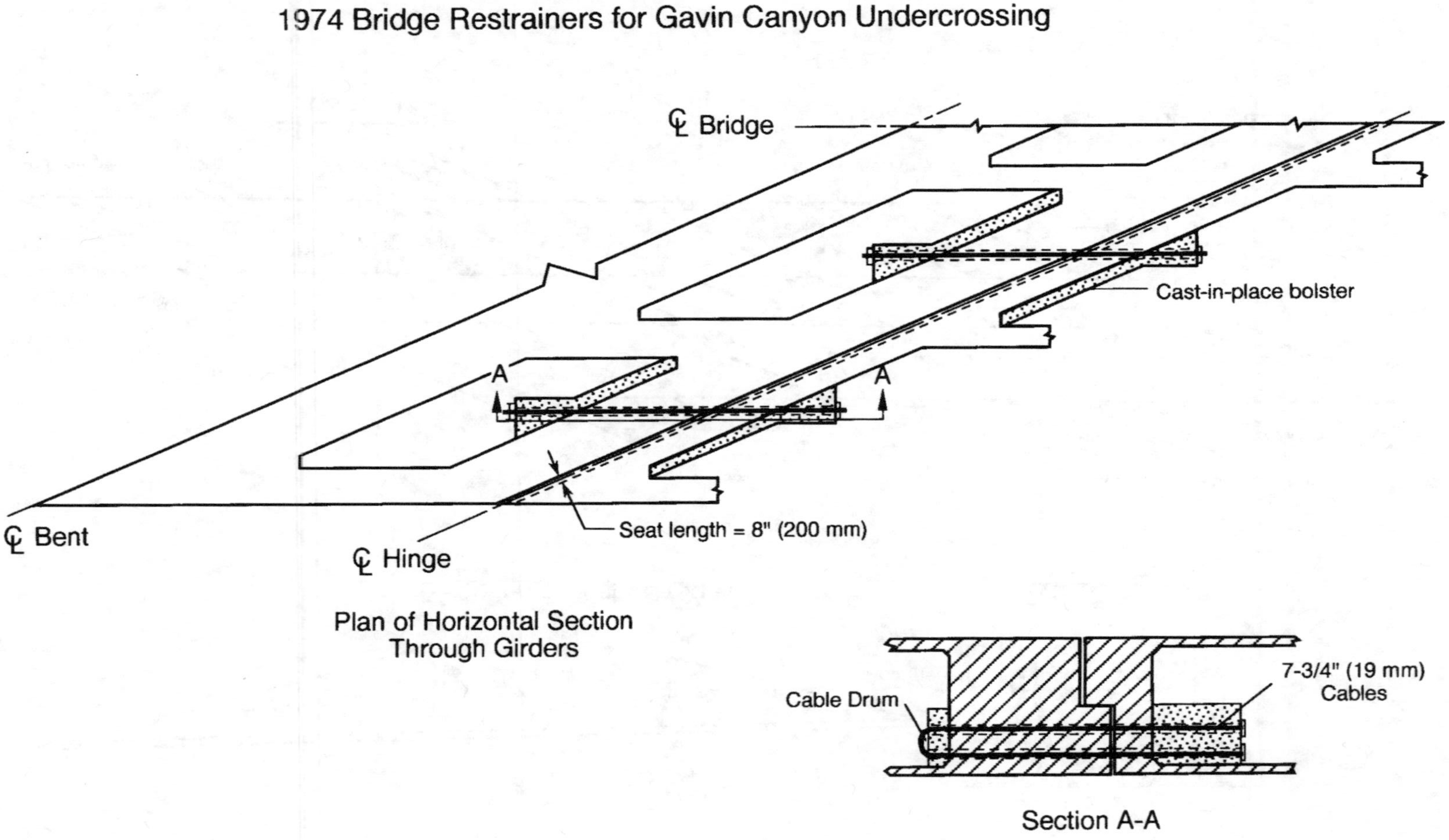

1974 Bridge Restrainers for Gavin Canyon Undercrossing

Ȼ Bridge

Cast-in-place bolster

Seat length = 8" (200 mm)

A

A

Ȼ Hinge

Ȼ Bent

Plan of Horizontal Section Through Girders

7-3/4" (19 mm) Cables

Cable Drum

Section A-A

Figure 4.5. Details of hinge restrainers of the Gavin Canyon Undercrossing.

4.3.2 State Route 14 (The Antelope Valley Freeway) Interchange with Interstate 5 (the Golden State Freeway)

Two bridges partially collapsed at this interchange: the Route 14/I5 Separation and Overhead Ramp C, which is the ramp linking westbound SR14 to southbound I5; and the North Connector Overcrossing Ramp M, which is the ramp linking westbound SR14 to northbound I5. The general layout of the interchange and the locations of the collapsed spans are shown in figure 4.6. In addition to the two collapsed ramps, there was evidence of pounding between spans at several hinges, and permanent differential offsets (both horizontal and vertical) were observed between the ends of the spans, as shown in figure 4.7. The cable restrainers installed at hinges in this interchange during the early 1970's may have been responsible for preventing further collapses during the Northridge earthquake.

This interchange was designed in 1968 and was under construction in 1971 when portions were damaged by the San Fernando earthquake. At that time, one of the completed ramps in the interchange collapsed, and two ramps which were under construction were damaged. The portion which collapsed in 1971 was the South Connector Overcrossing, connecting southbound I5 with eastbound SR14. A photograph of the collapsed ramp, taken in 1971, is shown in figure 4.8. This ramp was later rebuilt, with improved pier reinforcement, and it suffered no significant damage in the Northridge earthquake. The damaged portions of the other two ramps under construction in 1971 were repaired in place, but not strengthened; the portions not yet constructed were completed with limited seismic upgrading. Both of the ramps which partially collapsed in the Northridge earthquake were under construction at the time of the 1971 earthquake.

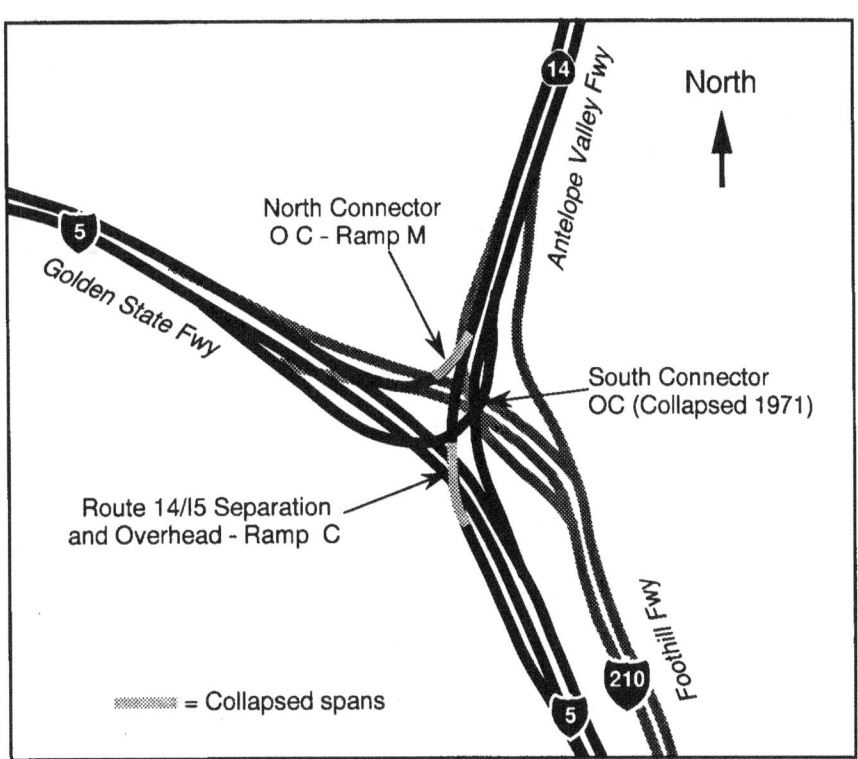

Figure 4.6. General layout of SR14/I5 interchange.

Figure 4.7.   Example of pounding and offset at a hinge in the SR14/I5 interchange.

Figure 4.8.   SR14/I5 interchange after the 1971 San Fernando earthquake. View looking to the west, showing collapsed South Connector Overcrossing.

This ramp was designed in 1968 and constructed in 1971. Plan and elevation views of this ramp are shown in figure 4.9. The structure consists of multiple-cell concrete box girders, most of which are post-tensioned, supported on single pier bents with flared tops. The portion of the ramp which collapsed was between Abutment 1 and the hinge located near Pier 4. A ground-level view of the collapsed span is shown in figure 4.11, and a view of damaged Pier 3 is shown in figure 4.12. The mode of failure of this ramp has not yet conclusively been determined, but the following scenario appears likely. Because Pier 2 was the shortest and stiffest pier in the structure, it probably attracted a large share of the horizontal seismic forces. The reinforcing details of the pier, shown in figure 4.10, indicate that the pier contained quantities of lateral reinforcement which would be considered inadequate by current standards. Thus it is likely that Pier 2 was damaged and collapsed, pulling the superstructure off the seat at Abutment 1[2]. It was reported that Pier 2 had completely disintegrated in the collapse. This observation is consistent with the conjecture that the pier was initially severely damaged in shear, and was then so badly weakened that it was crushed in compression. Following the collapse of Pier 2, a failure of the superstructure was initiated by excessive shear and negative bending moment at Pier 3. The superstructure sheared off on either side of Pier 3, leaving the pier standing nearly intact, as shown in figure 4.12. The span between Piers 3 and 4 then collapsed, pulling the superstructure off the hinge seat near Pier 4.

When the 1971 San Fernando earthquake occurred this ramp was under construction. Piers 2 and 3 had already been completed, and the bottom soffit and webs of the box girder between Abutment 1 and the hinge near Pier 4 had been cast and were resting on falsework. Settlement and shifting of the falsework resulted in damage to the parts of the ramp already constructed. After the San Fernando earthquake investigators noted cracking in the caps of Piers 2 and 3, consisting of cracks in the soffit slabs radiating 45 degrees from the pier corners, and vertical cracks in the box girder webs at the face of the pier cap, as shown in figure 4.13 [23]. It is not known how these cracks were treated in the repair work following the 1971 earthquake, or whether they were a contributing factor in the Northridge earthquake failure.

---

[2] It has been suggested that the superstructure was first pulled off the abutment seat, transferring excessive loads to Pier 2, causing it to fail. However, this appears unlikely as the bearing seat length at Abutment 1 was rather long: 24 inches (610 mm).

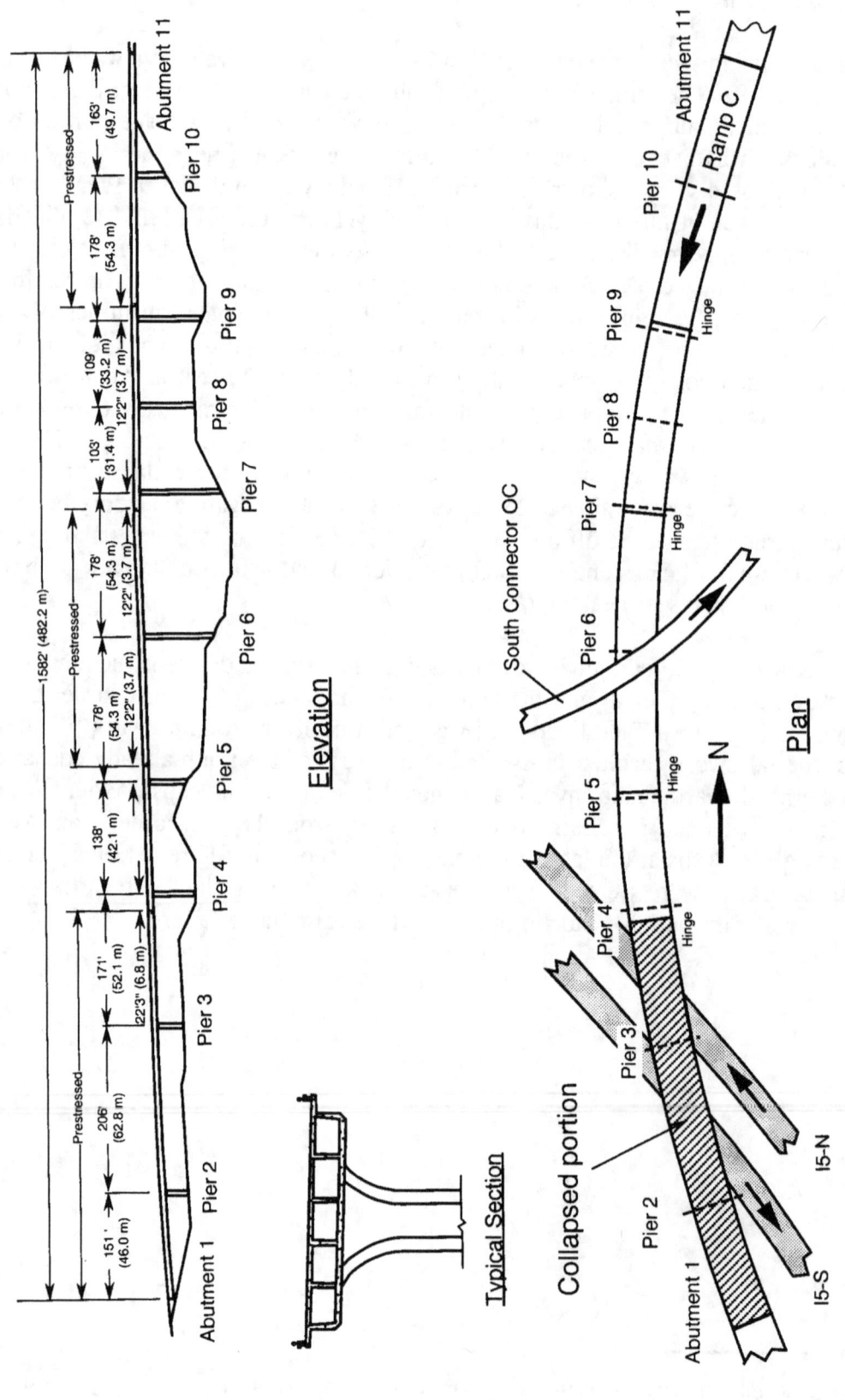

Figure 4.9. Plan and elevation views of the SR14/I5 Separation and Overhead, Ramp C.

90

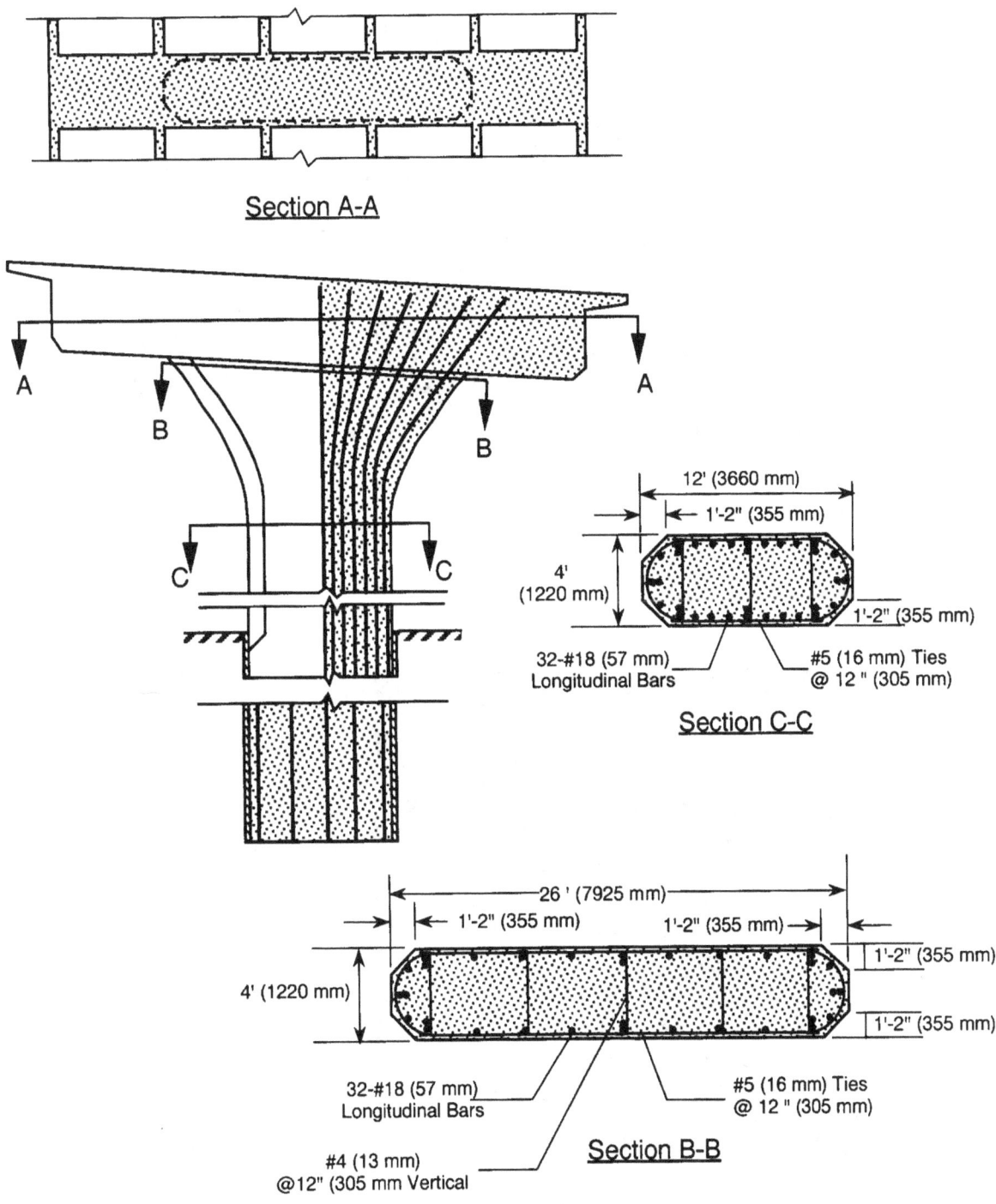

Figure 4.10. Details for Piers 2 and 3 of the SR14/I5 Separation and Overhead, Ramp C.

Figure 4.11. Overview of the collapse of the SR14/I5 Separation and Overhead, Ramp C, looking to the south at Abutment 1. Pier 3 can be seen at the right of the photograph (Photo courtesy of EERC).

Figure 4.12. Damage at Pier 3 of the SR14/I5 Separation and Overhead, Ramp C, looking to the west (Photo courtesy of EERC).

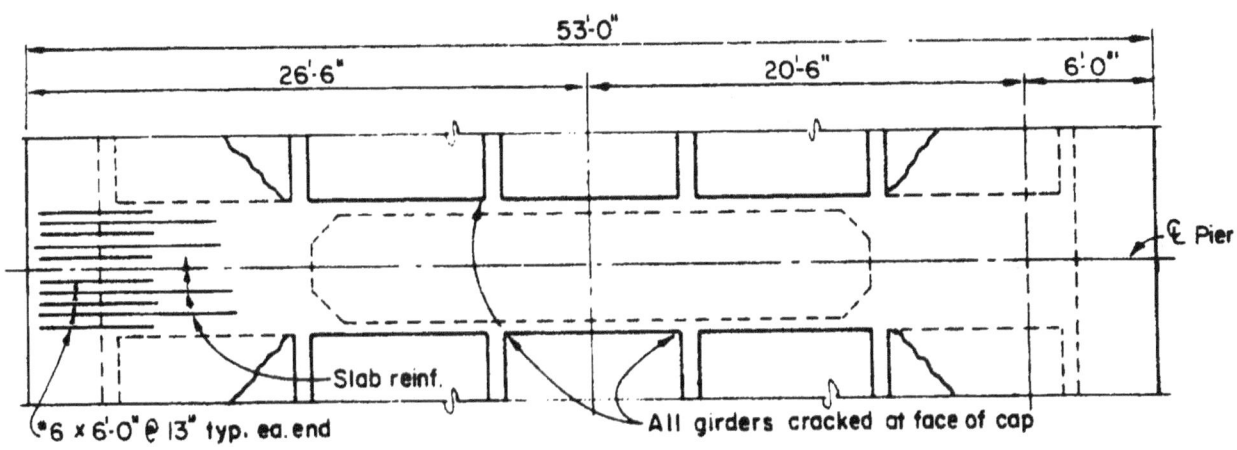

Figure 4.13. Cracking reported at Piers 2 and 3 following the 1971 San Fernando earthquake (reproduced from "The San Fernando Earthquake: Field Investigation of Bridge Damage," State of California, 1971).

4.3.2.2 *North Connector Overcrossing Ramp M*
Caltrans bridge No. 53-1964F

This ramp was designed in 1968 and constructed in 1971. Photographs of the collapsed portion of the ramp are shown in figures 4.14 and 4.15. Plan and elevation views of this ramp are shown in figure 4.17. The portion of the ramp which collapsed was located between Abutment 1 and Pier 3. As with the Separation and Overhead Ramp C, described above, this ramp was under construction in 1971. However, unlike Ramp C, this ramp was nearly completed when the San Fernando earthquake occurred. Only the portion from the hinge near Pier 8 to Abutment 11 remained to be constructed. The portion which collapsed in the Northridge earthquake, between Abutment 1 and Pier 3, was already constructed when the San Fernando earthquake occurred. Only minor damage to this ramp was reported following the 1971 earthquake [23]. This damage consisted of permanent offsets at the hinges near Piers 4 and 6.

The collapse in the Northridge earthquake appears to have been initiated by the failure of Pier 2. After Pier 2 failed, the simply supported span between Abutment 1 and the hinge near Pier 2 collapsed, and, as shown in figure 4.15, the superstructure failed near Pier 3 due to a large negative moment. Pier 2 completely disintegrated, as shown in figure 4.16. This is the shortest pier in the structure, so it is likely that it attracted a high level of lateral force, was damaged in shear, and finally collapsed in compression. Pier 10 is similar in height to Pier 1, but the quantities of lateral reinforcement in Pier 10 are greater than those in Pier 1, as shown in figure 4.18. This is because Pier 2 had already been completed, but Pier 10 had not yet been constructed, when the 1971 earthquake occurred. Following the 1971 earthquake the plans for Pier 10 were revised to provide increased lateral reinforcement, as shown in figure 4.18.

Figure 4.14. Collapsed portion of the SR14/I5 North Connector Overcrossing, looking east. Pier 2 was at the left, near the broken hinge on the ground (Photo courtesy of EERC).

94

Figure 4.15. View of the flexural failure at Pier 3 of the SR14/I5 North Connector Overcrossing, looking to the south.

Figure 4.16. View of crushed Pier 2 and the hinge near Pier 2 (Photo courtesy EERC).

95

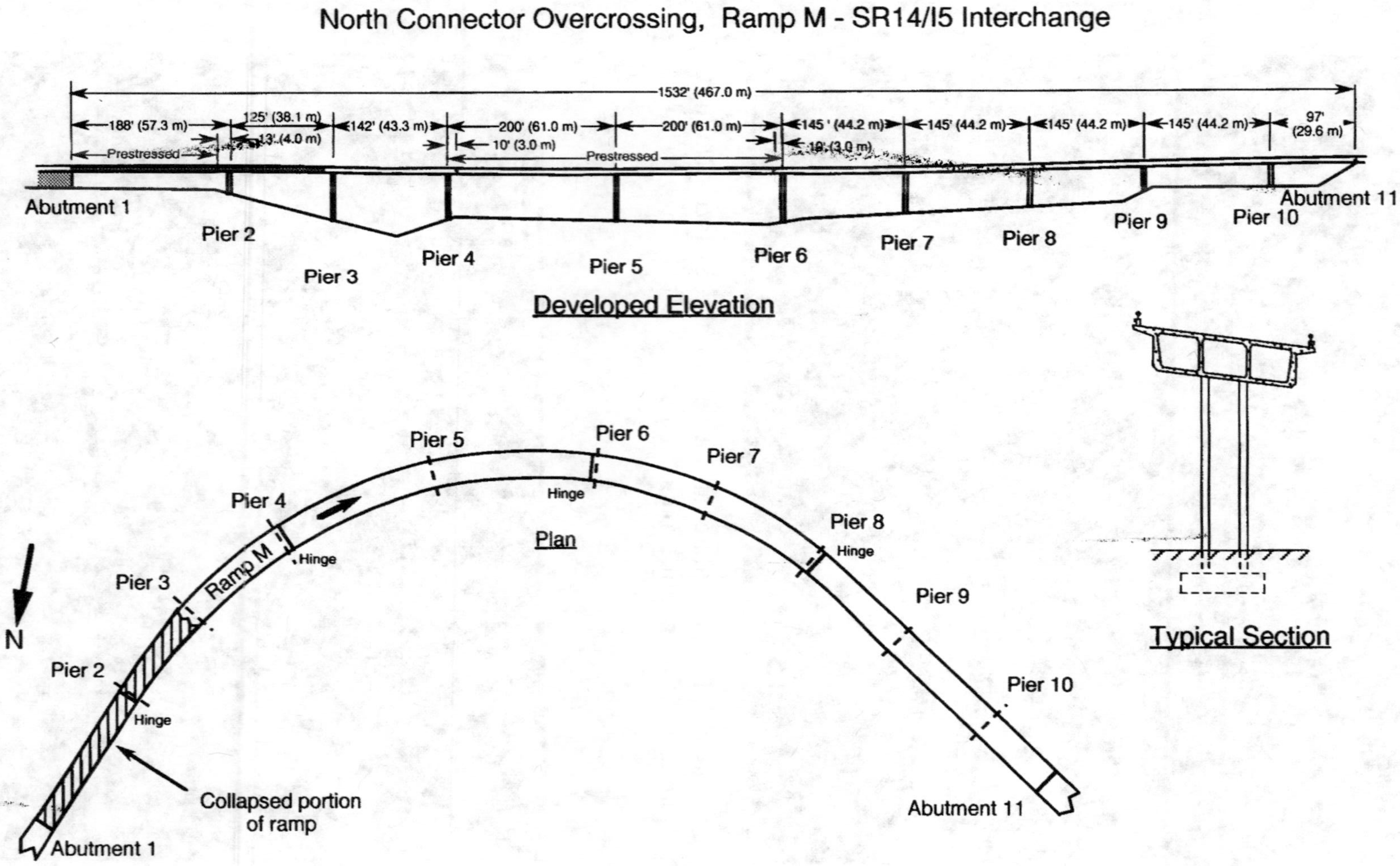

North Connector Overcrossing, Ramp M - SR14/I5 Interchange

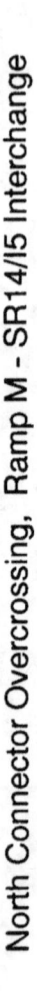

Developed Elevation

Typical Section

Plan

Figure 4.17. Plan and elevation view of the SR14/I5 North Connector Overcrossing.

96

SR14/I5 North Conncetor O C Ramp M - Pier 2

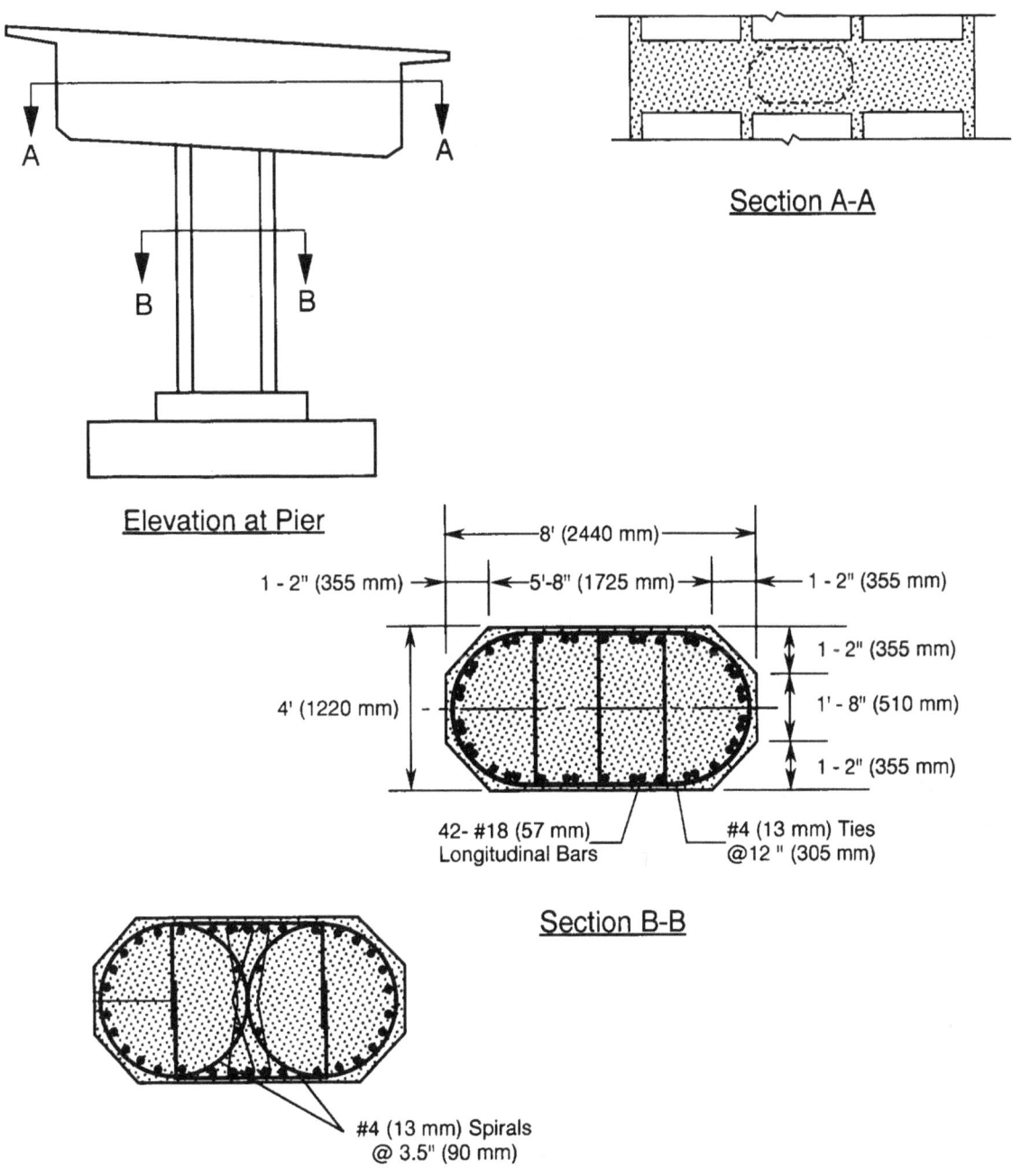

Section A-A

Elevation at Pier

8' (2440 mm)

1 - 2" (355 mm) → |←5'-8" (1725 mm)→| ← 1 - 2" (355 mm)

1 - 2" (355 mm)

4' (1220 mm)

1' - 8" (510 mm)

1 - 2" (355 mm)

42- #18 (57 mm) Longitudinal Bars

#4 (13 mm) Ties @12 " (305 mm)

Section B-B

#4 (13 mm) Spirals @ 3.5" (90 mm)

Pier 10 Reinforcement - 1972 Plans

Figure 4.18. Reinforcement details for Pier 2 of the SR14/I5 North Connector Overcrossing, Ramp M.

97

4.3.3 State Route 118 (The Simi Valley Freeway)

SR118 is the major east-west transportation route for northern Los Angeles County. It begins in the east at San Fernando, where it intersects Interstate 210 (the Foothill Freeway), and runs to Simi Valley in the west, passing just north of the epicentral region of the Northridge earthquake. The reconnaissance team inspected bridges on SR118 from Interstate 210 in the east, westward past the epicentral region, to White Oak Avenue. A number of bridges along SR118 received minor, repairable damage, but two bridges were damaged severely: portions of a bridge collapsed at the intersection of San Fernando Mission Boulevard and Gothic Avenue; and nearby there was severe pier damage and a near collapse of the bridge at Bull Creek Canyon Channel. The performance of these two bridges is described in detail below. In addition, two other bridges on SR118, which were less severely damaged, are described: the Ruffner Avenue Overcrossing and the Balboa Avenue Overcrossing.

As a result of the bridge damage at Mission-Gothic and Bull Creek Canyon Channel, SR118 was closed for about 2 weeks following the Northridge earthquake. Temporary repairs eventually permitted a partial re-opening of the westbound spans of SR118, however the traffic volume will be limited until both bridges can be replaced.

4.3.3.1 *State Route 118 (Simi Valley Freeway) at San Fernando Mission Blvd. and Gothic Ave. Caltrans bridge No. 53-2205*

An aerial view of the collapsed eastbound lanes of the Mission-Gothic Undercrossing is shown in figure 4.19. Because the Mission-Gothic Undercrossing was designed in 1972, after the San Fernando earthquake, the bridge contains seismic details which are improved over the details used in designs of the 1960's and earlier. Most notably, the spiral hoops in the bridge piers are spaced closely together, as shown in the pier details of figure 4.24. Nonetheless, the piers of the Mission-Gothic Undercrossing suffered severe damage in the Northridge earthquake, and one of the two parallel spans partially collapsed. Damage to piers at Mission-Gothic is shown in figures 4.20, 4.21 and 4.22. In addition to pier damage, there was also severe damage to the abutments, including cracked wing walls, settlement of soil behind the abutments, and apparent shifting of the abutments.

There are two notable features of this bridge which contributed to the damage caused by the Northridge earthquake: the geometry of the overall structure, and the geometry of the bridge piers:

The first important feature of the bridge is the its irregular geometry. Figure 4.23 shows that the plan shape of the bridge is a trapezoid. Thus, because of the orientations of the abutments, the structure was constrained to move in only one lateral direction during the earthquake, roughly to the southwest. Indeed, figures 4.21 and 4.22 show that the superstructure moved in this direction, creating a diagonal shear failures in many of the piers. There is also a highly irregular placement of piers, dictated in part by the trapezoidal plan shape of the bridge, and in part by right-of-way restrictions. The irregular plan shape and placement of piers created asymmetric stiffness and mass distributions, which undoubtedly lead to some piers being more heavily loaded than others during the earthquake. Detailed analyses will be required to determine how lateral earthquake loads were distributed among the piers.

The second, and perhaps more important, feature of this bridge is the geometry of the bridge piers. Pier details are shown in figure 4.24. The piers were all relatively short, roughly 7200 mm (24 ft) tall by 1800 mm (6 ft) across, making an aspect ratio of only 4:1. However the piers also featured architectural flares at the tops, roughly 3600 mm (12 ft) tall. These flares were intended to be non-structural features of the piers . It was believed that the flares would spall or otherwise deteriorate during earthquake loading so that they would not contribute to the bending stiffness of the piers. However, it is clear that in actual performance the flares created a zone of added stiffness, reducing the aspect ratio of the piers to approximately 3:1. Thus the piers were very stiff laterally, and were dominated by shear rather than bending. The detail at the footing/pier interface was also somewhat unusual for this bridge. Figure 4.24, section B-B, shows that the base of the pier rested inside a collar at the top of the pier footing. This detail was intended to permit free translation of the pier base during post-tensioning operations of the superstructure, before the collar was cast. The detail also had the effect of creating a hinge at the pier base. It is not immediately apparent whether this hinge improved or worsened the seismic performance of the bridge, although for a given lateral force the bending moments at the tops of the piers were greater than if the hinges at the bases of the piers had not been present.

The likely failure mode of the bridge was that the piers initially suffered severe shear damage, followed by crushing of a number of piers in compression. The structure may also have shifted to the southwest, as constrained by the geometry of the abutments. Although unseating at Abutment 5 did occur, this was probably a secondary effect, as the seat lengths were generous by current standards. Rather, failure was probably initiated by damage to the piers. In this case the failure of piers has important theoretical implications, as the piers of this bridge contained quantities of lateral reinforcement similar to those required by current seismic design standards. Therefore, further research will be required to determine why the pier reinforcement was inadequate in this case.

Figure 4.19.   Aerial view of the SR118 Mission-Gothic Undercrossing, looking to the north showing collapsed eastbound bridge (Photo courtesy of FHWA).

Figure 4.20.   Damage to piers of the SR118 Mission-Gothic Undercrossing, looking to the northwest at the north face of the westbound bridge, Bents 3 (foreground) and 2.

Figure 4.21. Damage to a pier of the SR118 Mission-Gothic Undercrossing, looking to the northwest at the southernmost pier of Bent 3 of the westbound bridge.

Figure 4.22. Damage to a pier of the SR118 Mission-gothic Undercrossing, looking to the west at Bent 4 of the eastbound bridge, which collapsed (Photo courtesy of EERC).

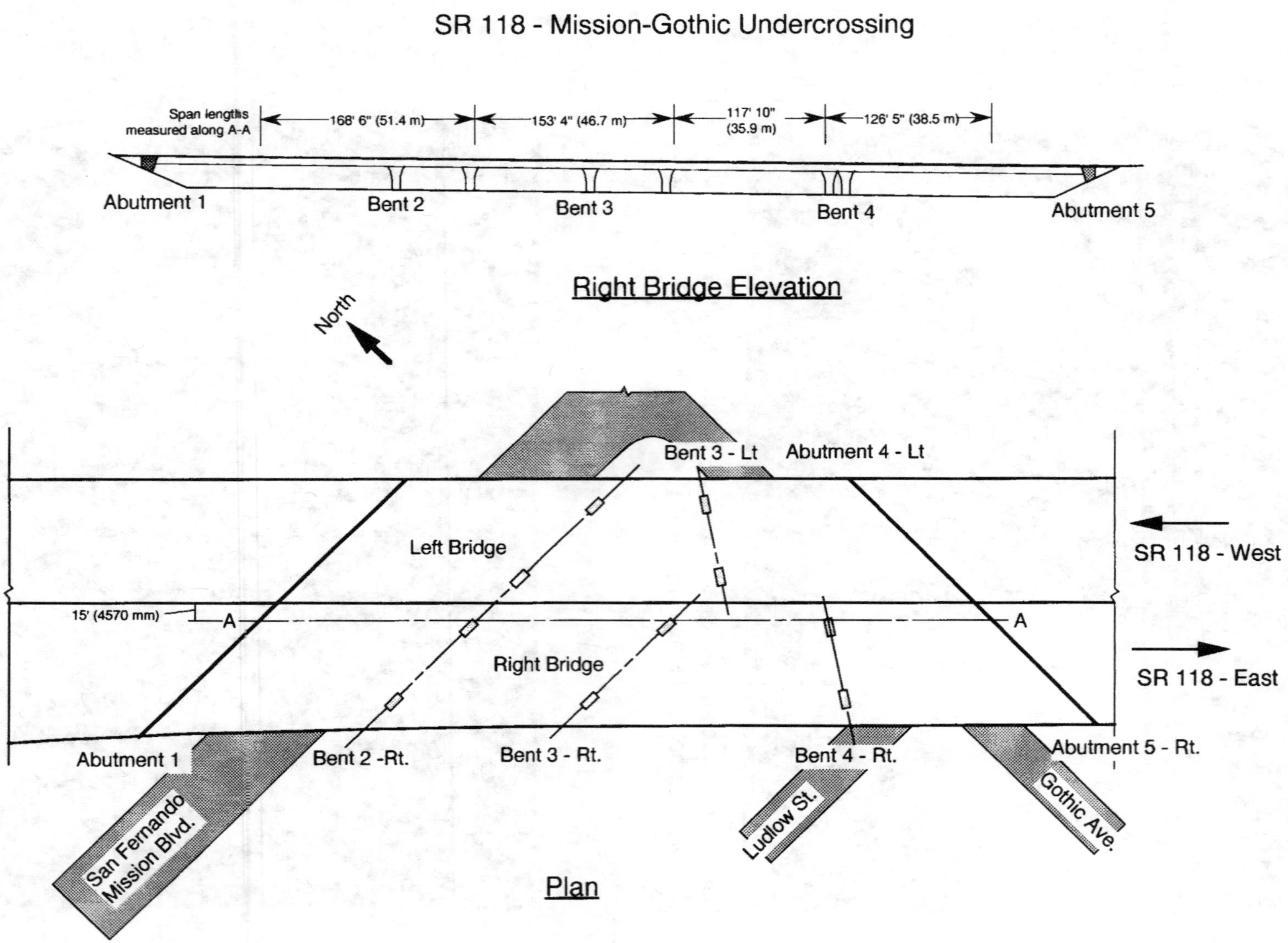

SR 118 - Mission-Gothic Undercrossing

Span lengths measured along A-A

Abutment 1 — 168' 6" (51.4 m) — Bent 2 — 153' 4" (46.7 m) — Bent 3 — 117' 10" (35.9 m) — Bent 4 — 126' 5" (38.5 m) — Abutment 5

North

Right Bridge Elevation

SR 118 - West

SR 118 - East

Abutment 5 - Rt.

Gothic Ave.

Abutment 4 - Lt

A

Bent 4 - Rt.

Ludlow St.

Bent 3 - Lt

Right Bridge

Bent 3 - Rt.

Left Bridge

Bent 2 - Rt.

15' (4570 mm)

A

Abutment 1

San Fernando Mission Blvd.

Plan

Figure 4.23. Plan and elevation views of the SR118 Mission-Gothic Undercrossing.

SR 118 - Mission-Gothic Undercrossing Pier Details

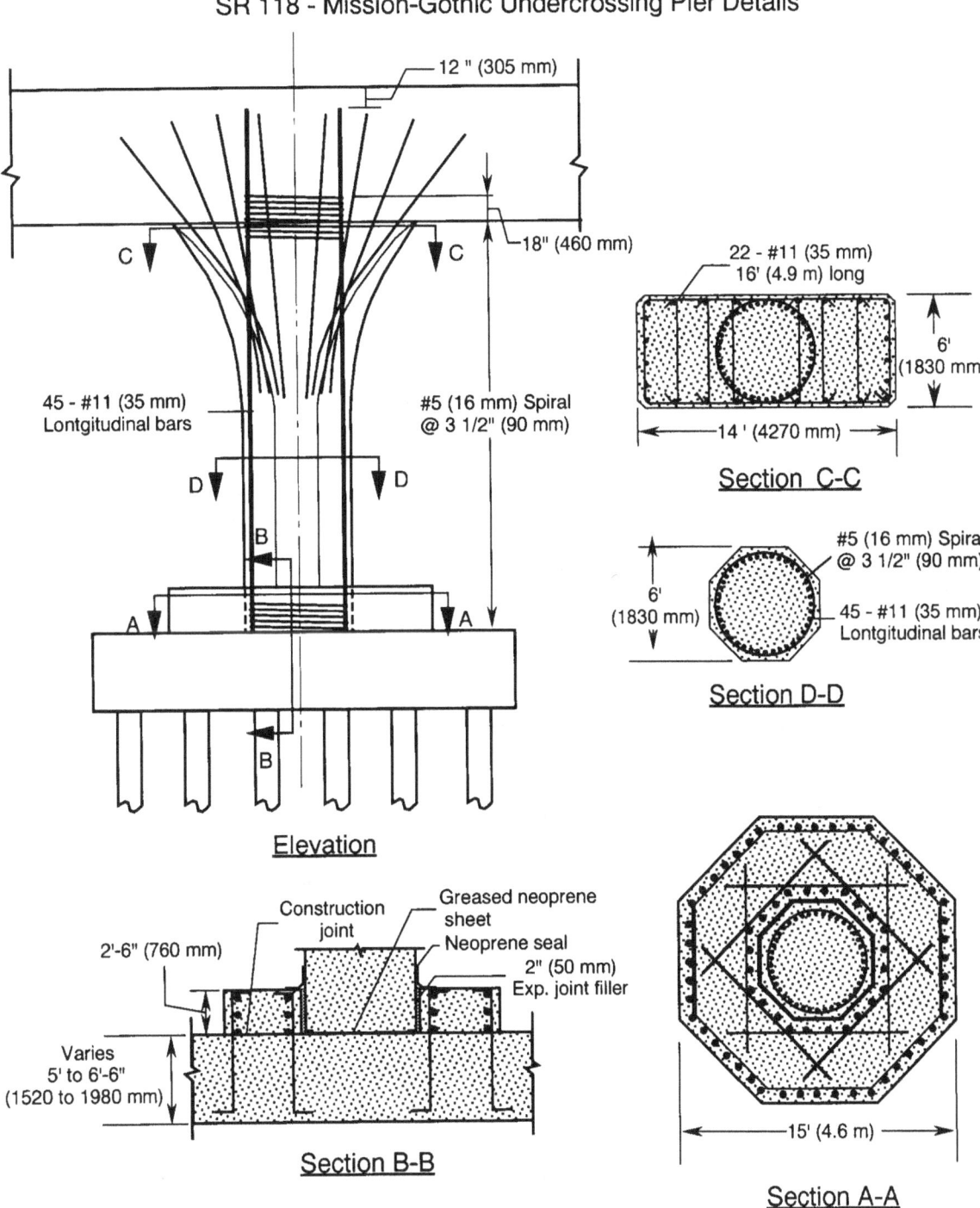

Figure 4.24. Pier details for the SR118 Mission-Gothic Undercrossing.

4.3.3.2 State Route 118 (The Simi Valley Freeway) at Bull Creek Canyon Channel. Caltrans bridge No. 53-2206

Figure 4.25 shows an aerial view, and 4.26 a ground-level view, of the SR118 bridge at Bull Creek Canyon Channel. The bridge did not collapse completely, but many of the piers were severely damaged, as shown in figures 4.27 and 4.28. In addition to pier damage, there was significant damage to the abutments, including cracked wing walls, settlement of soil behind the abutments, and possible shifting of the abutments. Plan and elevation views of the bridge are shown in figure 4.29, and pier details in figure 4.30.

This bridge was designed just after the 1971 San Fernando earthquake, so it contains some seismic detailing which is improved over earlier bridge designs. However, since it was not until several years after the San Fernando earthquake that seismic design codes for bridges were significantly changed, the design of this bridge would be considered substandard by current design codes.

All ten of the piers in Bent 3 failed in combined shear and compression near their bases, as shown by figures 4.27 and 4.28. In Bent 2, Piers on the south side of the span failed near their top end, as shown in the left foreground of figure 4.26, and the damage became progressively less for piers to the north in Bent 2. The farthest north piers in Bent 2 showed relatively little damage - only diagonal shear cracks near the base, with no spalled concrete. This uneven distribution of damage to piers was probably caused by the asymmetric plan geometry of the bridge, as shown in figure 4.29.

The confining reinforcement in the piers, shown in figure 4.30, is inadequate by current standards. Spiral confining hoops were spaced at 76 mm (3 in) near the top and bottom of each pier (presumably to provide confinement in potential plastic hinge regions), but the spacing was 305 mm (12 in) over most of the pier height. All pier failures occurred in the zone of wide spiral spacing. Another factor contributing to pier failure was that the effective lengths of the piers were much shorter than the distance between the footings and the girder soffit. The lengths of piers varied between roughly 6000 and 9100 mm (20 and 30 ft). In Bent 2, the effective pier lengths were decreased roughly one-third by compacted backfill soil above the pier footings. In Bent 3, the pier lengths were also decreased roughly one-third, but by a reinforced concrete channel liner wall, which was cast abutting the piers (fig. 4.30, section C-C). The shortened effective pier length resulted in stiffer piers, which were more susceptible to shear-dominated failure than bending-dominated failure.

Figure 4.25. Aerial view of State Route 118 at Bull Creek Canyon Channel, looking to the north (Photo courtesy of FHWA).

Figure 4.26. Ground-level view of State Route 118 at Bull Creek Canyon Channel, looking along the south edge, towards the east.

Figure 4.27. Damage to pier 3S-1 of State Route 118 at Bull Creek Canyon Channel, looking to the northwest.

Figure 4.28. Damage to piers of Bent 3S of State Route 118 at Bull Creek Canyon Channel, looking to the southeast.

SR 118 Bull Creek Canyon Channel Bridge

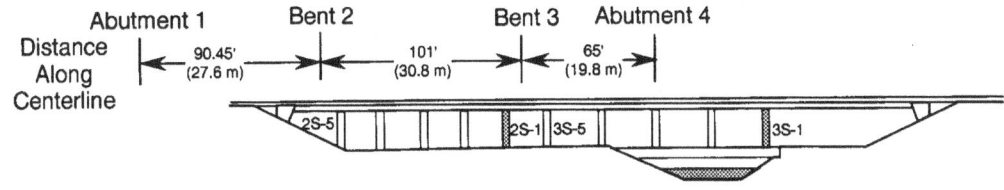

Elevation - Eastbound Bridge

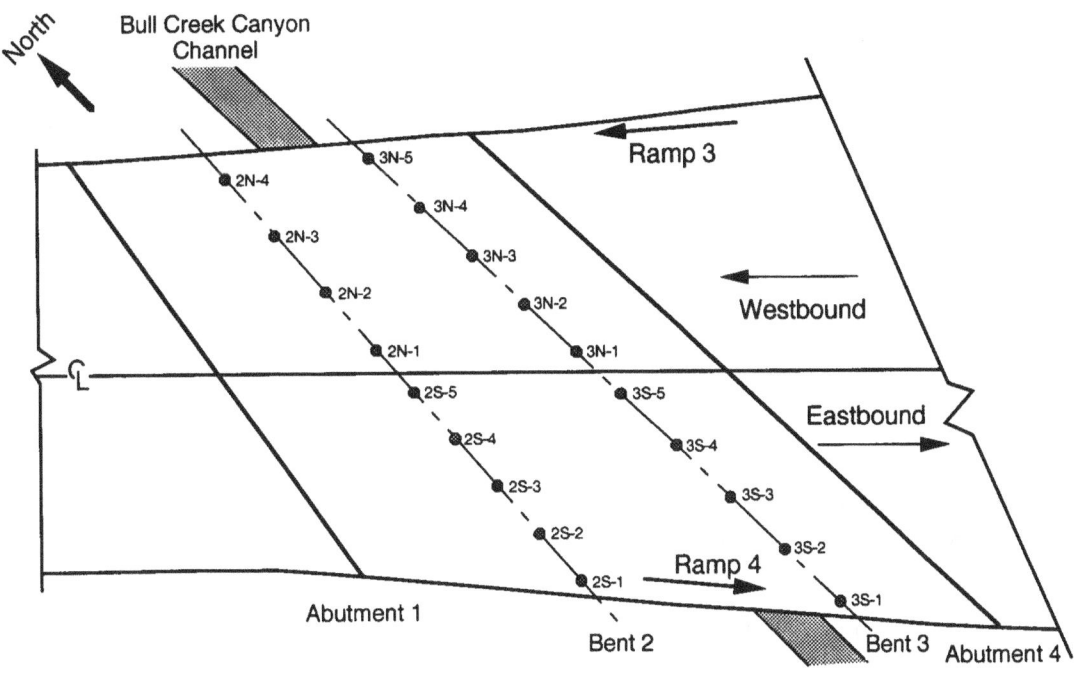

Plan

Figure 4.29. Plan and elevation views of State Route 118 at Bull Creek Canyon Channel.

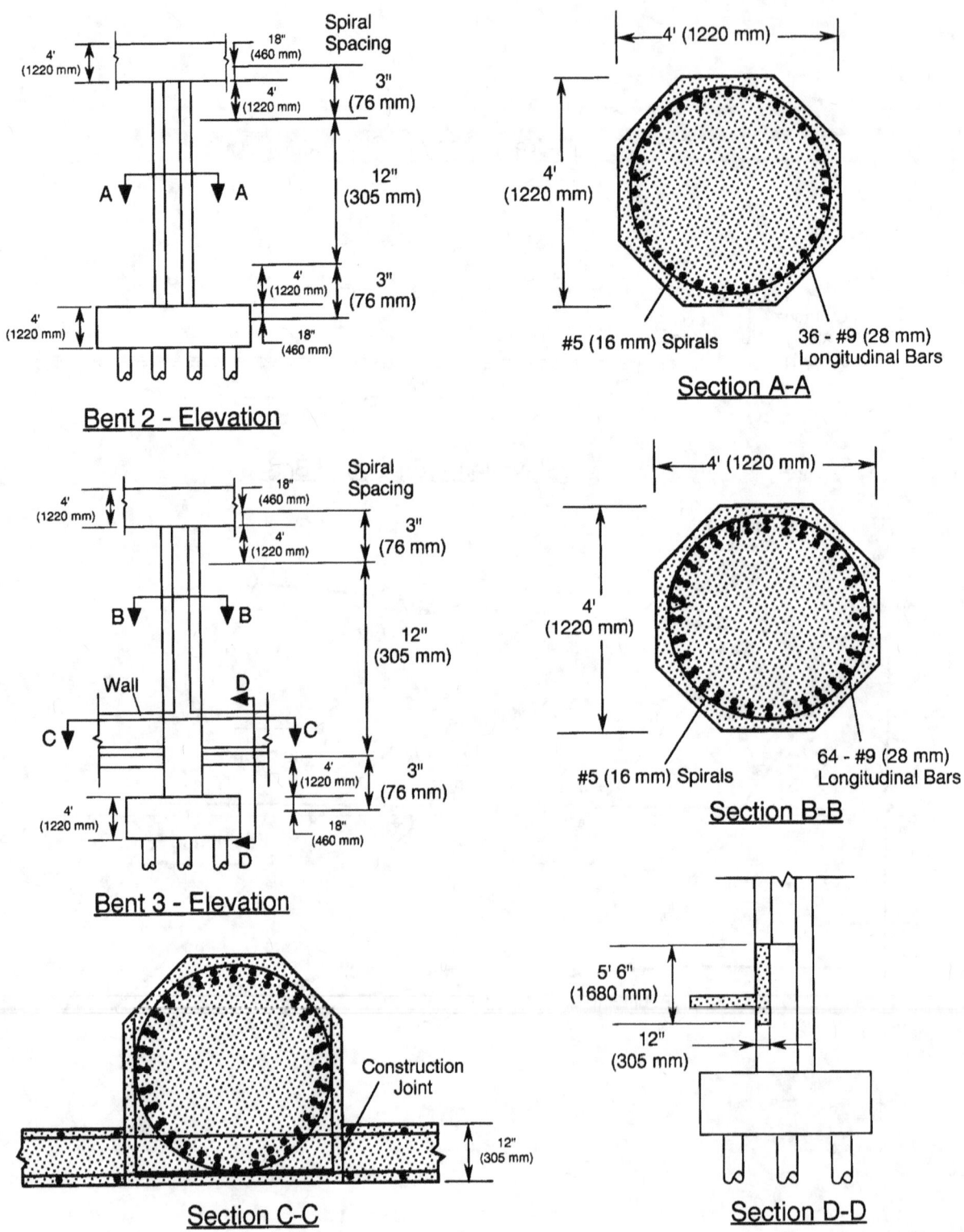

Figure 4.30. Pier details for State Route 118 at Bull Creek Canyon Channel.

4.3.3.3 State Route 118 (The Simi Valley Freeway) Ruffner Avenue Overcrossing Caltrans bridge No. 53-2396

This bridge was designed in 1971, after the San Fernando earthquake. It was not damaged seriously in the Northridge earthquake. The bridge has a fairly simple configuration: a two-span prestressed concrete box girder superstructure (spans of 50.3 m and 52.4 m [165 and 172 ft]), continuous over a central two-pier bent, with the superstructure resting on seats at each abutment. The seat lengths were generous: approximately 1500 mm (5 ft). The bridge alignment is skewed about 21 degrees. The only significant damage suffered by the bridge was extensive spalling at one of the central piers, as shown in figure 4.31. The pier damage appeared to be limited to the cover concrete. This pier could be repaired relatively easily, and the bridge returned to full service. The spiral hoop reinforcement in the piers was #5 (16 mm) spirals spaced 89 mm (3.5 in), which is similar to the level of confining reinforcement required by current design codes. It is interesting to note that these piers have similar geometry and reinforcement content as the piers at the nearby Mission-Gothic Undercrossing, which were severely damaged. However, these piers are more flexible because they are taller and have a somewhat smaller diameter than the piers at the Mission-Gothic Undercrossing.

The good seismic performance of this bridge can probably be attributed to two factors. First, the central piers performed well because they contained adequate confining reinforcement and they were slender enough that they were not prone to a shear-dominated failure mode. Second, the overall geometry of the bridge is fairly compact, so that much of the lateral forces were carried by the abutments rather than the central piers. It is not common to see extensive seismic damage to short-span overpasses of this type.

Figure 4.31. SR118 Ruffner Ave. Overcrossing, easternmost central pier, looking to the west.

4.3.3.4 State Route 118 (The Simi Valley Freeway) Balboa Avenue Overcrossing

This bridge is a two-span overpass, very similar to the Ruffner Avenue Overcrossing, described above. The two bridges are located only a few hundred meters apart on SR118. The Balboa Avenue Overcrossing suffered very little damage due to ground shaking, except for some minor spalling at the tops of the central piers. (Although there was considerably more spalling of cover concrete of the piers of the Ruffner Avenue Overcrossing, the degree of damage to both bridges was relatively minor, and the response of the two bridges to ground shaking could be considered similar).

During the earthquake a water main, which was contained inside the bridge superstructure, ruptured. The water released by the broken main flowed under and around the south abutment, and caused extensive erosion on both the east and west flanks of the abutment. Soil was washed away beneath about one-third of the abutment foundation. The top ends of abutment piles were visible on both flanks of the abutment. A view of the washout on the east flank of the abutment is shown in figure 4.32.

Figure 4.32. SR118 Balboa Avenue Overcrossing, view of the washout on the east side of the south abutment, caused by a ruptured water main.

4.3.4 Interstate 10

Interstate 10 is a major east-west artery running between Santa Monica and downtown Los Angeles. The freeway was constructed in 1966. Major bridge collapses occurred at two locations: (1) the La Cienega Blvd.-Venice Blvd. Separation and (2) the Fairfax Ave.-Washington Blvd. Undercrossing.

Between the two bridges which collapsed, I10 passes over Ballona Creek. Figure 4.33 is a view looking toward the southwest of the spans over the creek. There was essentially no damage to the supporting piers. Adjacent to the bridge over Ballona Creek, there is a westbound ramp which exits from I10 to Cadillac Ave. A portion of this ramp is supported by single piers which have been retrofitted with steel jackets, as shown in figure 4.34. No damage was noted to these retrofitted piers. The Cadillac Ave. ramp represents the only case known to the authors where undamaged retrofitted piers were located close to major collapse sites. However, because the retrofitted Cadillac Ave. ramp piers were immediately adjacent to an older, non-retrofitted multispan bridge which was undamaged (the Ballona Creek overpass), it is not known whether the Cadillac Ave. ramp piers were subjected to the same levels of lateral forces as piers at the two collapse sites at La Cienega-Venice and Fairfax-Washington.

4.3.4.1 Interstate 10 La Cienega Blvd./ Venice Blvd. Separation, Caltrans Bridge No. 53-1609

Figure 4.35 is an aerial view of I10 where it passes over La Cienega Blvd. and Venice Blvd. The view is toward the south, and Venice Blvd. is the diagonal street on the left side of the photograph. The portion of the westbound lane which collapsed to ground level can be seen. However, there was extensive damage to most of the supporting piers of the eastbound and westbound lanes.

Figure 4.36 shows elevation and plan views of the nine-span bridge structure. Solid wall piers provided support adjacent to the abutments, and the remainder of the supports were multiple-pier bents. Two expansion joints (hinges) were provided as shown. Bents 3 to 7 included three supporting piers for each lane, while Bent 8 had four piers per lane. The exit ramp to La Cienega Blvd. and the eastbound collector-distributor did not collapse. Figure 4.37 shows the pier details. The piers had circular cross sections with a diameter of 1220 mm (4 ft), and the longitudinal reinforcement consisted of #11 (35 mm) or #18 (57 mm) deformed bars. The different pier reinforcement configurations were identified by pier "types" as shown in figure 4.37. These pier types are indicated in the plan shown in figure 4.36. The lateral reinforcement consisted of #4 bars (13 mm) at 305 mm (12 in) vertical spacing.

Figure 4.38 is a ground-level view of the portion of the westbound lane that collapsed to the ground at the hinge located between Bents 7 and 6. The pier in the foreground is the northernmost pier of Bent 7. It is seen that there was extensive column shortening due to the failure of the lateral reinforcement to provide adequate confinement of the core concrete. Fractured lateral reinforcement can be seen to the right of the failed portion of the pier. Figure 4.39 shows the other two piers of Bent 7 which supported the westbound lane. Extensive failure and column shortening is evident. The concrete block wall behind the piers is part of a storage building that was constructed beneath the bridge structure. The storage building extended from

111

Venice Blvd. to La Cienega Blvd. The piers of Bent 7 which supported the eastbound lane suffered relatively minor damage, and the roadway to the east of Bent 7 remained largely at its original elevation.

Figure 4.40 shows the northernmost pier of Bent 6, located just to the west of the hinge. This pier totally disintegrated, but the storage building prevented the roadway from collapsing to the ground. Figure 4.41 shows the southernmost pier supporting the eastbound lane at Bent 3. The top of the pier is severely damaged and it is likely that the storage building prevented the total collapse of the roadway.

In summary, the bridge structure spanning La Cienega Blvd. and Venice Blvd. was extensively damaged. The failure is attributed to the small amount of lateral pier reinforcement. As the piers cracked due to the lateral loading, the lack of adequate confinement resulted in a reduction of the vertical load capacity because of core concrete loss and buckling of the longitudinal bars. Had it not been for the storage building located beneath the bridge, it is likely that more spans would have collapsed to the ground.

Figure 4.33. I10 Bridge over Ballona Creek, looking to the southwest.

112

Figure 4.34. Cadillac Ave. ramp; view to east showing jacketed pier.

Figure 4.35. Aerial view (looking south) of I10 Separation at La Cienega Blvd. and Venice Blvd., (Photo courtesy of FHWA).

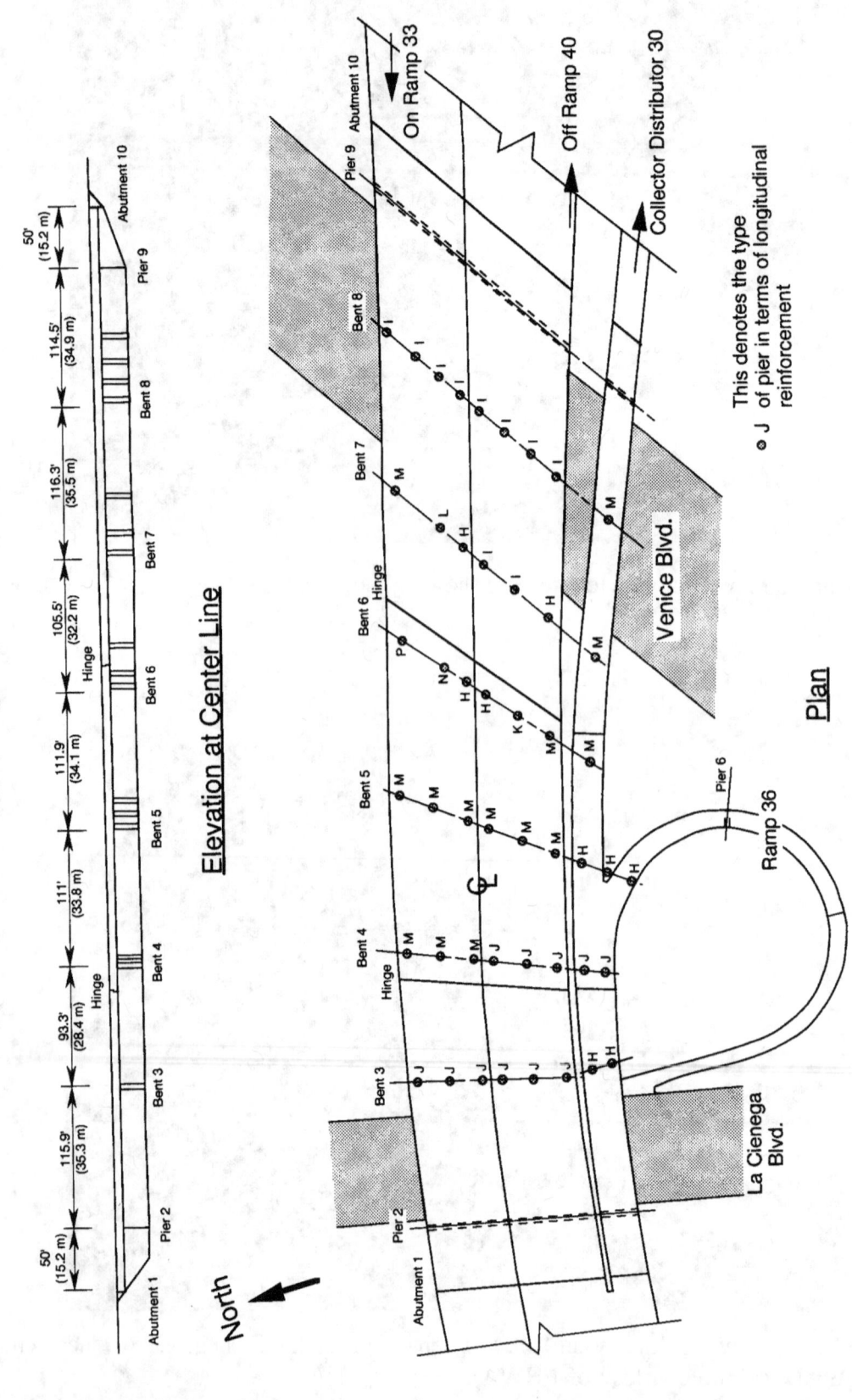

Figure 4.36. Elevation and plan of I10 Separation at La Cienega Blvd. and Venice Blvd.

114

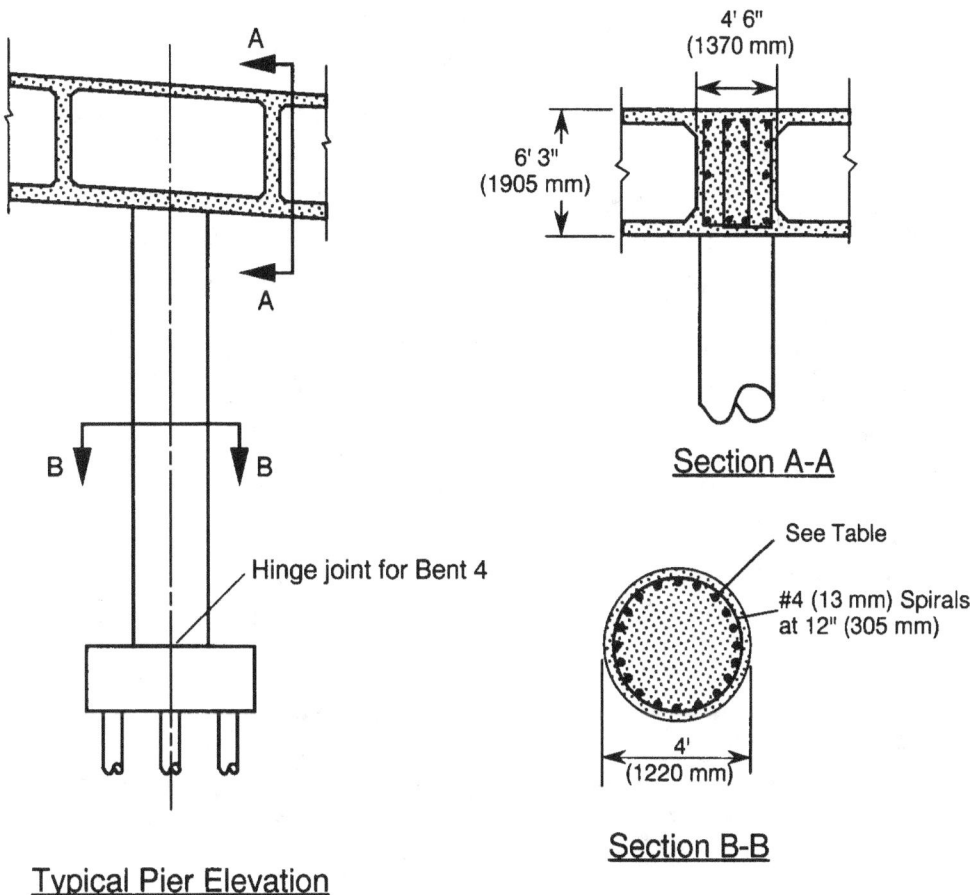

I-10 La Cienega-Venice Separation Pier Details

4' 6"
(1370 mm)

6' 3"
(1905 mm)

Section A-A

A

A

B

B

Hinge joint for Bent 4

Typical Pier Elevation

See Table

#4 (13 mm) Spirals
at 12" (305 mm)

4'
(1220 mm)

Section B-B

Longitudinal Reinforcement

Type	Bar Size	No. of Bars
H	#11 (35 mm)	12
I	#11 (35 mm)	18
J	#11 (35 mm)	24
K	#11 (35 mm)	36
L	#11 (35 mm)	42
M	#11 (35 mm)	48
N	#18 (57 mm)	20
P	#18 (57 mm)	24

Figure 4.37. Pier details for I10 Separation at La Cienega Blvd. and Venice Blvd.

Figure 4.38.   Collapsed westbound lane of I10 at Venice Blvd.; pier of Bent 7 in foreground.

Figure 4.39.   Failed piers in Bent 7 supporting westbound lane of I10 at Venice Blvd.

Figure 4.40. Northernmost pier of Bent 6 supporting westbound lane of I10 (west of Venice Blvd.).

Figure 4.41. Piers of Bent 3 supporting eastbound lane of I10 at La Cienega Blvd.

4.3.4.2 Interstate 10 Fairfax Ave.-Washington Blvd. Under Crossing
Caltrans bridge number 53-1580

Figure 4.42 shows the elevation and plan of the Fairfax Ave.-Washington Blvd. Undercrossing. The eastbound and westbound lanes of I10 were supported by solid wall piers adjacent to the abutments and by multiple-pier bents at the remaining locations A construction joint (hinge) was located to the west of Bent 4. Because of the skewed alignment of I10 relative to Washington Blvd., the westbound lane of I10 was designed with an additional bent (Bent 4A) compared with the eastbound lane. The piers were of circular cross section with a diameter of 1220 mm (4 ft). The longitudinal reinforcement consisted of #11 (35 mm) deformed bars. The number of longitudinal bars in each pier is shown adjacent to the pier locations in figure 4.42. It can be seen that the piers in Bent 4 had significantly more longitudinal bars compared with the other piers. The lateral reinforcement was #4 (13 mm) bars at a vertical spacing of 305 mm (12 in).

The earthquake caused partial collapse of two spans of the eastbound and westbound lanes on either side of Bent 3 (fig. 4.42). When the reconnaissance team arrived at the site, the collapsed spans had been completely removed and workmen were preparing to open up traffic on Fairfax Ave. Hence it was not possible to examine the collapsed structure. Conversations with Caltrans engineers at the site revealed that the piers in Bent 3 had failed and caused the girders to sag at this location. However, cable restrainers at the hinge west of Bent 4 prevented the girders from falling off of the hinge seats (fig. 4.43). Figure 4.44 is a photograph provided by EERC which shows the westbound lane of I10 over Fairfax Ave. It can be seen that the piers in Bent 3 shortened and caused the girder to sag. It can also be seen that the span to the west of Pier 2 lifted off of the abutment. Figure 4.45 is a close up view of one of the piers in Bent 3. The failure mode is similar to that observed at Venice Blvd. and La Cienega Blvd. When the piers were subjected to lateral ground motions, the lateral reinforcement was not able to adequately confine the core concrete. As a result of lateral load damage, there was a loss of axial load capacity and the piers shortened under the action of the vertical loads. As mentioned, the piers at Bent 4 had considerably more longitudinal reinforcement than the other piers. Examination of the piers in Bent 4 revealed varying degrees of diagonal cracking and spalling of the concrete cover. At the time of the site visit, these piers were surrounded with wooden shoring as a precautionary measure during the demolition of the collapsed spans.

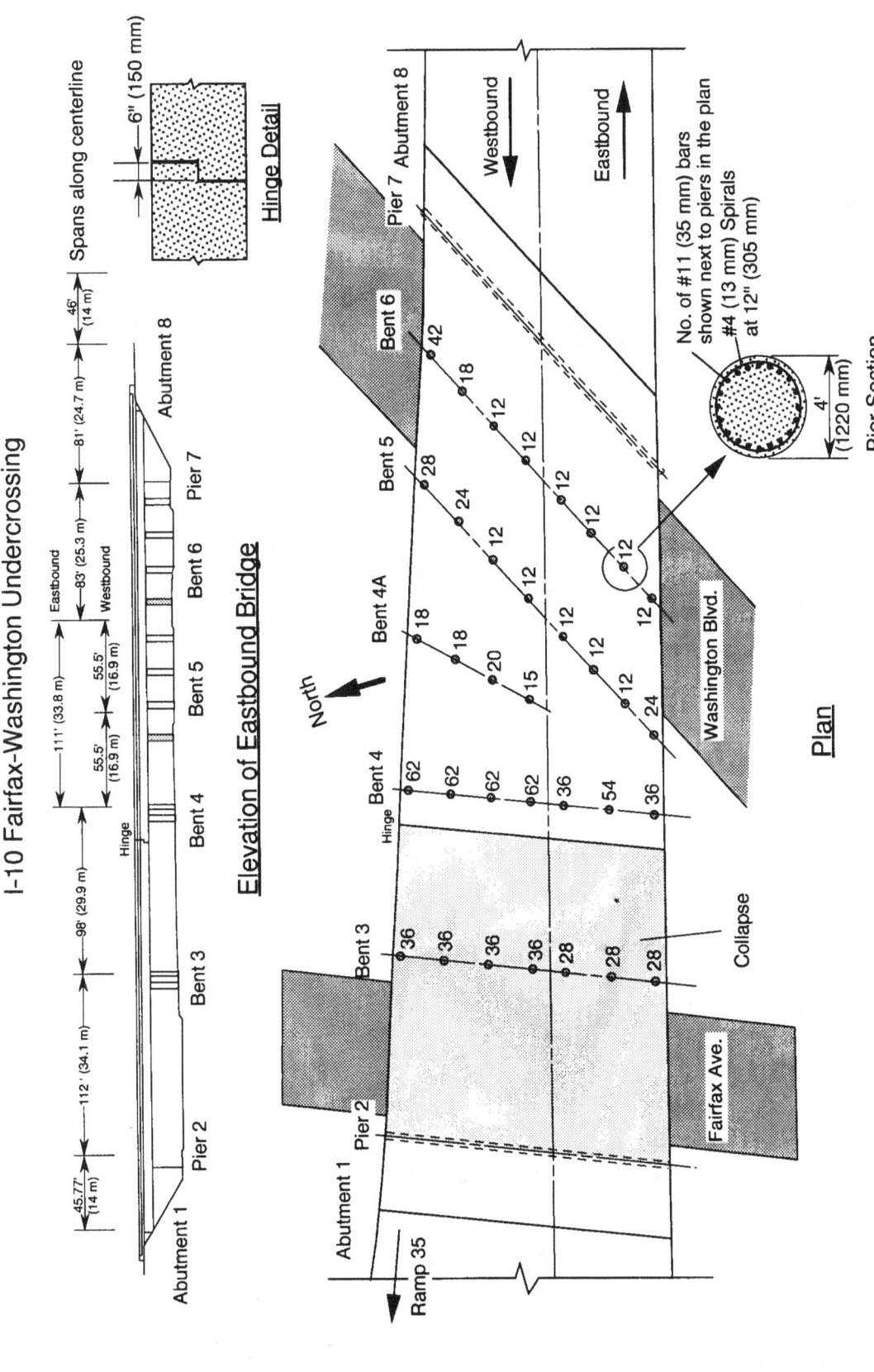

Figure 4.42. Elevation and plan of I10 at the Fairfax Ave./Washington Blvd. Undercrossing.

Figure 4.43. Hinge adjacent to Bent 4 of I 10 at Fairfax Ave.; cable restrainers prevented loss of support (Photo courtesy of EERC).

Figure 4.44. View of collapsed span of I10 over Fairfax Ave.; note rotation of girder over Pier 2 (Photo courtesy of EERC).

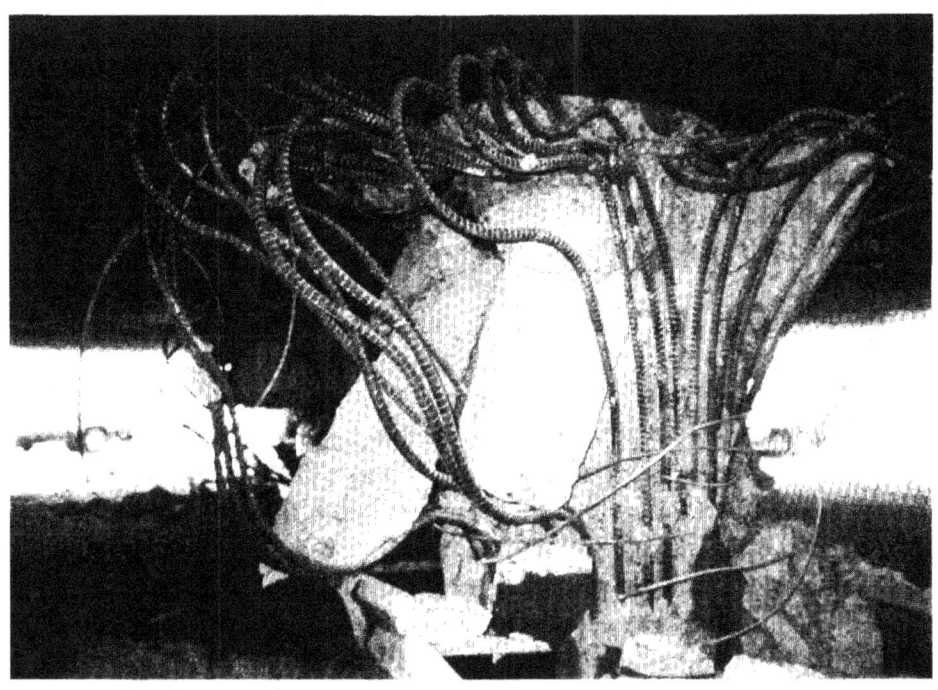

Figure 4.45.   Failed column in Bent 3 of I10 at Fairfax Ave. (Photo courtesy of EERC).

4.3.5 Bearing Damage at State Route 134 (The Ventura Freeway) / US101 (The Hollywood Freeway) Interchange
Caltrans bridge No. 53-1339P

The interchange of the Ventura Freeway and Hollywood Freeway was designed in the late 1950s. The eastbound and westbound lanes of the Ventura Freeway pass over the northbound and southbound lanes of the Hollywood Freeway. The bridges are made of multiple-cell reinforced concrete box girders supported by multiple-pier bents. At the abutments, the girders are supported by sliding-type bearings or rocker-type bearings. Examination of some of the accessible bearings of the eastbound lane of the Ventura Freeway revealed serious damage.

Figure 4.46 shows a simplified plan of the eastbound lane of the Ventura Freeway and the Riverside Drive ramp. Figure 4.47 is a ground level view of the eastbound lane as seen from the northbound lane of the Hollywood Freeway. At Abutment 1 (fig. 4.46), bearing supports are provided at the locations of the webs in the box girder. As shown in figure 4.46, the longitudinal axes of the bearings are aligned at right angles to the longitudinal axes of the girder webs. The four bearings on the north side of the eastbound lane of Ventura Freeway are of the sliding-type. Figure 4.48 shows the type of damage that was observed at these locations. Apparently, the dynamic frictional resistance of the bearing resulted in forces sufficient to spall off the shell of the abutment. The remainder of the bearings supporting the eastbound lane and the Riverside Drive ramp are of the rocker type. Figure 4.46 shows a schematic of this type of bearing. A steel bearing block with cylindrical surfaces is located between steel plates set into the abutment and girder end diaphragm. The blocks are kept in position with a system of guide plates and restraining plates as shown in figure 4.46. All of the rocker bearings showed some type of earthquake damage. The bolts for the restraining plates were sheared off at many locations, and the sheared bolt heads were found at distances of up to several meters from their original position. Some of the bearing blocks were skewed from their original positions (fig. 4.49). In one case, the bearing block had tipped over resulting in a complete loss of support at that location (fig. 4.50).

These observations highlight the unsuitability of rocker-type bearings to withstand the effects of seismic deformations. Because of redundancy, the failure of one bearing may not result in serious damage to the supported girder. However, multiple bearing failures could drastically alter the forces in the girder, and these forces could exceed the girder capacity.

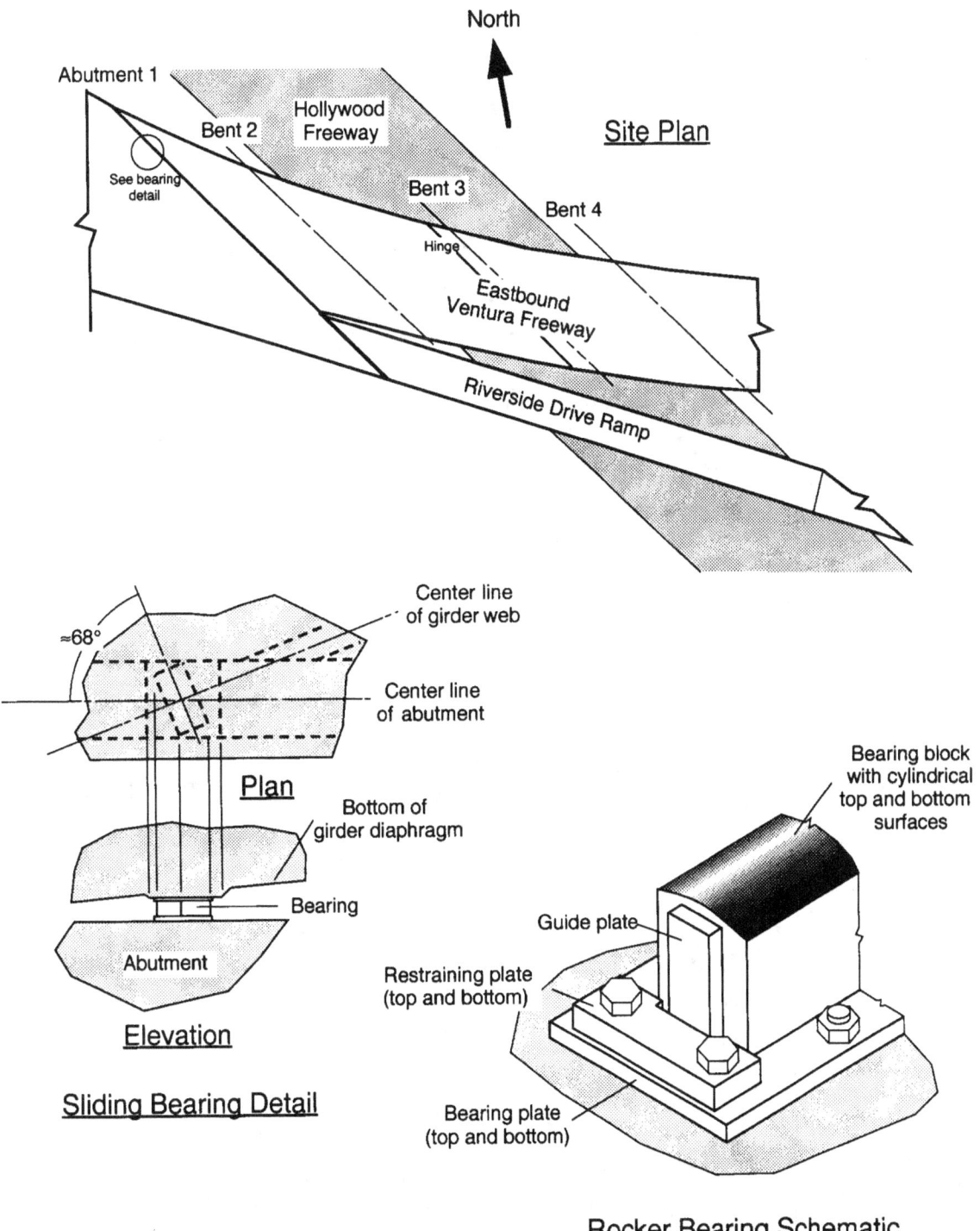

Figure 4.46. Eastbound lane of Ventura Freeway crossing over Hollywood Freeway; site plan and bearing details.

123

Figure 4.47. Eastbound lane of Ventura Freeway as seen from the northbound lane of Hollywood Freeway.

Figure 4.48. Abutment damage at sliding-type bearing.

Figure 4.49. Displaced bearing block in rocker-type bearing.

Figure 4.50. Bearing block tipped over at this location resulting in loss of support to girder.

4.3.6 Interstate 5 (The Golden State Freeway), State Route 118 (The Simi Valley Freeway), Southwest Connector
Caltrans bridge number 53-2329

This is a long, curved ramp structure with piers of varying height. The last pier before the west abutment, adjacent to Sharp Avenue, exhibited severe shear cracking. This was one of the shortest and stiffest piers in the structure, so it probably attracted large lateral forces. Damage to the pier is shown in figures 4.51 and 4.52. Note that when the photos in figures 4.51 and 4.52 were taken the loose cover concrete had been removed by Caltrans workers to inspect damage to the core. It appeared that cracks extended into the core of the pier. The pier is octagonal in cross section, measuring 2440 mm (8 ft) across, and has a flared section at the top. Longitudinal reinforcement consists of 64 #11 (36 mm) bars (EERC 1994). This pier contains high levels of shear reinforcement: #4 (13 mm) spirals spaced at 89 mm (3.5 in). Damage to the abutment just to the west of this pier was also observed. This damage was apparently due to pounding between the superstructure and the abutment.

Figure 4.51.   View of the westernmost pier at the Interstate 5, State Route 118, Southwest Connector, looking to the southeast. Loose cover concrete has been removed by Caltrans.

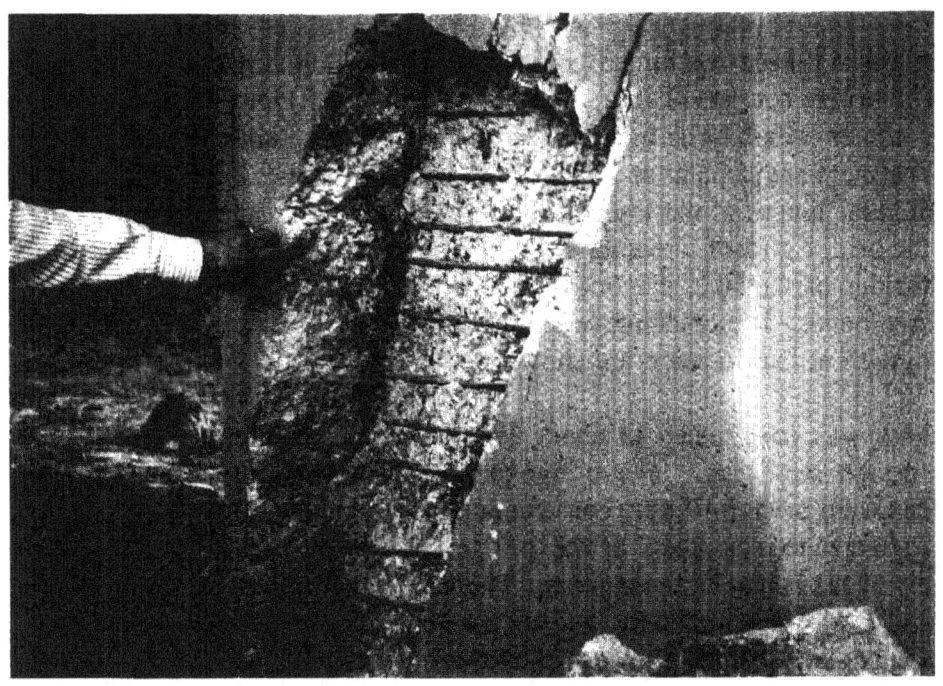

Figure 4.52. Close-up view of the westernmost pier at the Interstate 5, State Route 118, Southwest Connector, looking to the southeast. Loose cover concrete has been removed by Caltrans.

4.3.7 State Route 90 (Marina Freeway) / Interstate 405 (San Diego Freeway) Interchange, Jefferson Blvd. Undercrossing
Caltrans bridge number 53-1255

This is a cast-in-place reinforced concrete bridge which carries Interstate 405 over Jefferson Blvd. The bridge consists of four spans: two 8.5 m (28 ft) long end spans and two 16.0 m (52.5 ft) long center spans. The bridge is supported on three six-pier bents, making a total of 18 piers. The piers are circular and 1220 mm (4 ft) in diameter. All but two of the eighteen piers have structural hinges at the top of the pier footing. The outer piers of each bent are located outside the bridge girders, creating an "outrigger" configuration, as shown in figure 4.53. After the Northridge earthquake, diagonal cracks were observed in all six outrigger joints at the ends of the three bents. The cracking was most serious on the east end of the center bent. A close-up photograph at that location are shown in figure 4.54.

This bridge was constructed in about 1961, so generally speaking it does not meet current seismic design standards. The bridge is somewhat unusual because in the original design allowances were made for future construction of the ramps of the SR90/I405 interchange passing overhead: the outermost piers of the bridge were more heavily reinforced to allow for later extensions of the height of those piers. The reinforcement in the exterior piers consisted of 22 #18 bars (57 mm) longitudinally, and #5 bar (16 mm) spiral hoops spaced at 114 mm (4.5 in); the inner piers were reinforced with 14 #9 bars (29 mm) longitudinally, and #4 (13 mm) spirals spaced at 305 mm (12 in). The exterior piers were later extended in height, as can be seen in figure 4.53. It is not clear how structural continuity was achieved between the original exterior piers and the pier extensions, since no explicit provisions were made in the original design for extending the longitudinal reinforcement.

The damage observed in the Northridge earthquake possibly arose from three factors. First, the joint regions where cracking occurred are not as heavily reinforced as they would be under current design standards. Second, the structural hinges at the bases of most outrigger piers tended to increase the moments imposed on the outrigger joints. Third, the Jefferson Blvd. Undercrossing shares piers with the SR90 ramp above, as shown schematically in figure 4.55. The upper SR90 structure is more flexible than the lower Jefferson Blvd. Undercrossing, possibly resulting in further concentrations of moments at the outrigger joints.

Figure 4.53. Overview of the outrigger joint at the SR90/I405 interchange, Jefferson Boulevard Undercrossing, center bent, west side, looking to the north.

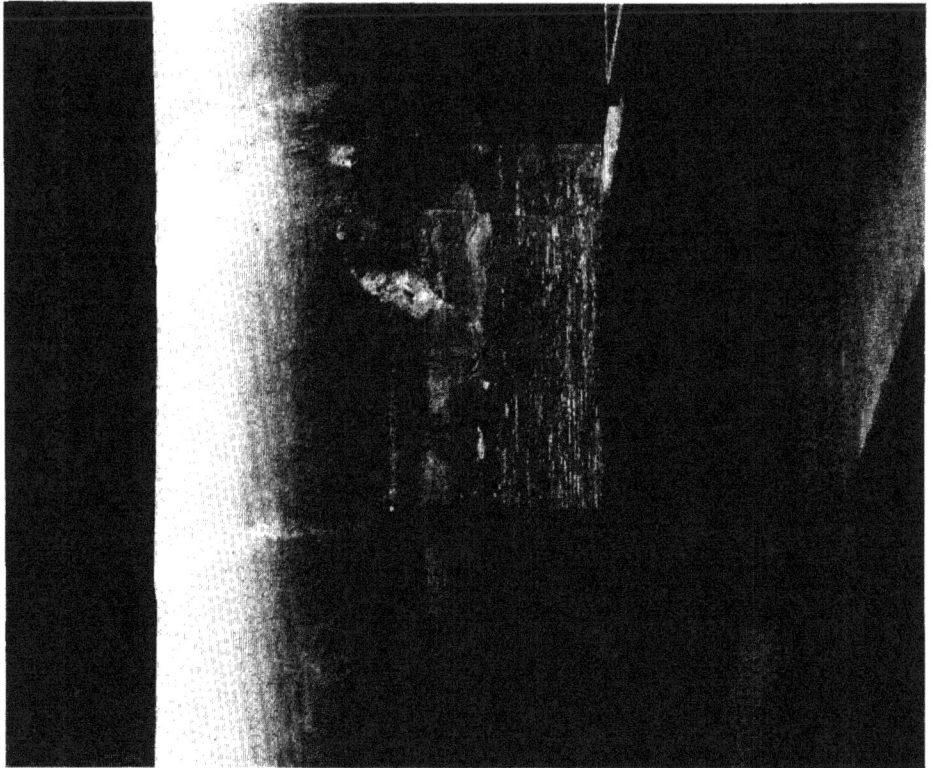

Figure 4.54. Close-up of the outrigger joint at the SR90/I405 interchange, Jefferson Boulevard Undercrossing, center bent, east side, looking to the south.

129

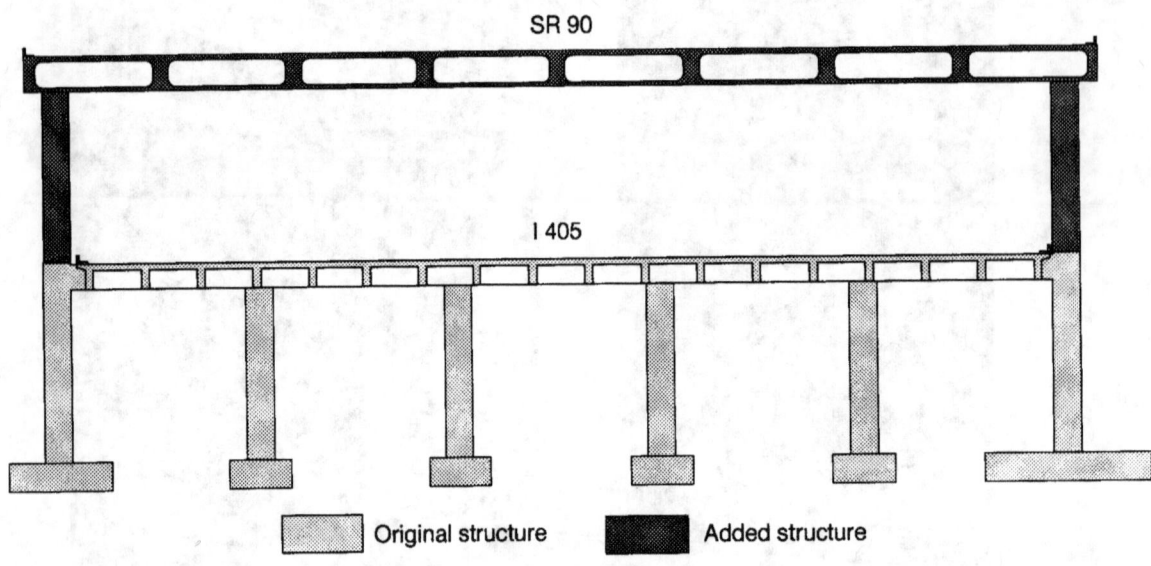

Figure 4.55. Schematic cross section, showing columns shared by SR90 and the Jefferson Boulevard Undercrossing.

4.3.8 Abutment Damage

There were many bridges which suffered no damage, or very minor damage, to the bridge structure itself - the superstructure, piers, and pier foundations - but which experienced damage to the abutments. Abutment damage is not widely reported because it usually does not threaten to cause collapse of a bridge. Nonetheless, repairs to abutments can be costly and disruptive. The seismic performance of bridge abutments is not well understood. Seismic design, evaluation and retrofit methods for abutments require further study.

In the Northridge earthquake, bridge abutment damage ranged from minor settlement of backfill soil at the approaches, to cracking of wing walls, to permanent displacement of the entire abutment. For example, at the intersection of State Route 118 and Interstate 210, there was damage to the abutment at the east end of the long elevated structure connecting eastbound SR118 with northbound I210. An overview of the abutment is shown in figure 4.56, and a close-up of some of the abutment sidewall cracking is shown in figure 4.57. At the interchange of US101, SR134 and SR170, at the Riverside Drive Offramp Overcrossing (Caltrans bridge No. 53-1493S, described above) the abutments at both ends of the offramp exhibited severe cracking in the wing walls. Damage to concrete abutment piles was reported [5] at the Las Virgenes Overcrossing on US101 (Caltrans bridge No. 53-1442). There were many other cases of bridge abutment damage observed by the reconnaissance team, and reported by other investigators, which are too numerous to list here.

Figure 4.56. Overview of abutment at the east end of the ramp connecting eastbound SR118 with northbound I210.

Figure 4.57. Close-up of abutment wall cracking at the east end of the ramp connecting eastbound SR118 with northbound I210.

4.3.9 Other Bridge Damage

The reconnaissance team inspected the sites of major bridge damage, however, other damage sites have been reported by other investigation teams. A brief summary of the nature of the damage is provided below.

4.3.9.1 Interstate 5/Interstate 210 Interchange

The 8-span southwest connector (bridge number 53-1989F),which carries traffic from East I210 to South I5, was supported by single piers. Both abutments were damaged. At the north abutment (Abutment 9), there was horizontal and vertical offset between the approach slab and the bridge girder. The damage is attributed to failure of the transverse shear keys [24]. In addition, there was some pounding damage where Pier 4 passes through the girder of the San Fernando Rd. elevated structure. At the south abutment (Abutment 1), there was evidence of pounding damage and twisting of the girder. Spalling was also observed in several piers [5].

The following damage was also observed where I5 crosses over San Fernando Rd. [5]:
- pounding damage at the abutments,
- pounding damage at hinges,
- pullout of girder at abutments,

132

- ○ wing wall damage, and
- ○ spalling at the tops of the piers in the multiple-pier bents.

4.3.9.2 *Interstate 405/Interstate 10 interchange*

At this interchange, I10 passes over I 405, and connectors pass over I 10. In 1990, piers were retrofit with steel jackets, hinge restrainers were added, and foundations were strengthened [5]. It was found that there was evidence of movement and pounding at the hinges and there was a seat failure at a hinge supported by a drop bent cap. No damage was observed in the retrofitted piers.

4.3.9.3 *Santa Clara River Bridge*

Interstate 5 crosses the Santa Clara River by means of two, skewed, seven span bridges, one in each direction (bridge number 53-0687). The bridges are composed of steel plate girders with composite concrete decks. The girders are simply supported by wall piers and abutments. Reported failure included the following [5]:
- ○ failure of anchor bolts attaching the girders to the wall piers,
- ○ spalling of concrete wall piers at girder anchorages,
- ○ failure of cables in the cable restrainer assemblies.

4.3.9.4 *Las Virgenes Road Overcrossing at Ventura Freeway*

The overcrossing was originally built in 1961 as a two-lane bridge (53-1442). In 1974, the bridge was widened with the addition two lanes. The four-span bridges are composed of steel plate girders with a composite concrete deck. The girders are supported on multiple-pier concrete bents. The reported damage included the following [5]:
- ○ pounding damage at hinges,
- ○ abutment fill settlements of about 100 mm (4 in), and
- ○ damage (cracking and spalling) to the top end of a concrete pile supporting the south abutment; the pile was excavated after the earthquake for inspection.

4.4 Summary

1) On the whole, bridges performed well in the Northridge earthquake. Nonetheless, there were several failures which proved to be extremely disruptive to automobile traffic in the region. There will be large and immediate economic costs for the repair or replacement of the bridges which were heavily damaged. Perhaps more costly, however, will be the long-term indirect economic costs due to disruptions in transportation patterns throughout metropolitan Los Angeles. This highlights the critical importance of highway bridges to the economic and social vitality of the region, and the need to press forward with seismic retrofit and seismic research programs.

2) Generally speaking, bridges designed using standards developed after the late 1970's performed very well. Most bridges that were severely damaged were designed earlier. While this implies that the current seismic design standards for bridges are adequate, we should not be lulled into a false sense of security. For example, the SR118 bridge at Mission-Gothic was designed in 1973 with piers containing high levels of spiral confining reinforcement, similar to the levels of confining steel that would be specified today. Yet these piers failed catastrophically, possibly because they were short and stiff, and because architectural flares at their tops further increased their stiffness. It is also important to bear in mind that despite the good performance of many bridges in this earthquake, we cannot yet predict the level of damage to bridges which would be caused by an earthquake with a larger magnitude (around 8.0) or which would be more centrally located in the Los Angeles area.

3) Unusually high vertical accelerations were recorded at several locations near bridge structures during this earthquake. Further research is required into the influence of such high accelerations on the performance of bridges, and on whether or not high vertical accelerations were a contributing cause of bridge failures in this earthquake.

4) Although there were few reports of significant damage to older bridges which had been seismically retrofit, it is not clear that this earthquake provided a conclusive test of the performance of various retrofit methods. For example, the cable restrainers of one bridge - the Interstate 5 bridge at Gavin Canyon - were unable to prevent parts of the bridge deck from falling off the supports. Further evaluations of cable restrainers design criteria, and seat retrofit methods may be necessary. Detailed studies of how jacketed piers and reinforced foundations performed in this earthquake should be carried out. It should be determined how severely this earthquake tested field applications of these techniques, so that they can continue to be employed with confidence.

5) Older bridge bearings, of the steel rocker type, are highly susceptible to damage in strong ground shaking. Rocker bearings are inherently unstable under lateral loading. Loss of rocker bearing support can lead to a broad range of bridge damage, including cracked girders, loss of roadway elevation alignment, and complete collapse of the superstructure. Rocker bearings are widely used in the Central and Eastern United States. Since there is an increasing awareness of the potential for damaging earthquakes in these regions, it should be a national priority to study the performance of rocker bearings and methods for retrofitting or replacing them.

6) Bridges which were damaged often had skewed alignments or irregular plan configurations.

Damage to skewed bridges was exemplified by the performance of the I5 bridge at Gavin Canyon, and the SR118 bridges at Mission-Gothic and at the Bull Creek Canyon Channel. The potential for seismic damage to bridges having skewed or irregular alignments was known before this earthquake, yet relatively little has been done to address this problem.

7) Failures were often associated with short bridge piers. Example include the failures at the I5/SR14 interchange, on SR118 at Mission-Gothic, and the I5/SR118 Southwest Connector. In these cases the piers were not only short, but they were also flared at the top, creating a zone of increased stiffness, decreasing the effective pier length. The piers at the I5/SR14 interchange contained low levels of confining reinforcement by today's standards. However, the piers on SR118 at Mission/Gothic, and at the I5/SR118 Southwest Connector, contained high levels of confining reinforcement, and they still failed. Thus, there may be problems with short piers in general, whether or not the confining reinforcement meets current standards. A better understanding of the seismic performance of short piers, including piers with flares, is needed. In addition, the role short piers play in the overall seismic response of bridge structures, particularly those structures with a mixture of short and tall piers, needs to be investigated further.

8) Many of the bridges damaged in the earthquake had multiple-pier bents. To date, because of the obvious seismic vulnerability of single-pier bents, most seismic retrofit efforts have been directed towards retrofitting isolated piers; comparatively little has been done to address the strengthening of multiple-pier bents. Further research is required to develop cost-effective seismic retrofit guidelines for multiple-pier bridge bents.

9) The failure of the water main contained within the Balboa Boulevard overpass at SR118 highlighted an important secondary function of bridge structures: bridges often carry utilities such as power, water, gas and telephone lines, which are critical to the emergency response and well-being of a community following a major earthquake. Guidelines and standards need to be established for the safe routing of utility lines within bridges.

10) There was widespread damage to bridge abutments. The seriousness of this damage ranged from minor backfield settlement, to cracked wing walls, to shifting of entire abutment structures. Relatively little is known about the seismic behavior of bridge abutments, particularly the interaction between soils and the abutment structure. Further research is needed to develop methods for the design of effective earthquake-resistant bridge abutment structures.

CHAPTER 5

PERFORMANCE OF LIFELINE SYSTEMS

5.1 Introduction

Lifelines include water, sewer, gas, fuel, electric power, telecommunications, and transportation systems. These systems are critical to the vitality of the built environment and the functioning of modern society. They provide services to the community to maintain its safety, health, and economic activities. Damaged lifelines can impede emergency response following an earthquake, and can hinder postearthquake recovery. Disruption of regional lifeline systems due to a major natural disaster such as an earthquake can have a profound effect on the entire nation because of the economic interdependence of lifeline systems and the functions they support.

The Northridge earthquake is expected to be the costliest natural disaster this country has experienced to date. A significant portion of those losses is due to the loss of function of lifeline systems and the cost for their repair and replacement.

This chapter offers a brief overview of the performance of lifeline systems, including observations made by many investigators, but with particular emphasis on the sites that the team visited personally. Gratitude is extended to the reconnaissance team members of the American Society of Civil Engineers Technical Council for Lifeline Earthquake Engineering, many of whom also served on the EERI reconnaissance team. In regard to transportation systems, this chapter addresses only the performance of airports and railways. The performance of highway bridges is presented in chapter 4.

5.2 Water and Wastewater Systems

Water supply from local sources has always been a problem for Southern California. In addition to limited sources from the region's local groundwater basins, the main water supply is from Northern California and the Colorado River. January 17, 1994 was the first time in history that an earthquake resulted in the breakage of all four pipelines that feed water to the region's three water treatment facilities.

Compared with the extensive damage caused by the 1971 San Fernando earthquake to the Jensen treatment plant in Sylmar (under construction at the time), the 1994 earthquake caused only minor damage. The 1994 damage included lateral spreading of the ground or soil settlement around the facilities, leaks in pipelines, and leaks at construction joints. While water supply to these facilities was available once the major pipelines were repaired, the system nevertheless failed to provide water to customers because of damage to the water supply distribution network, especially the network serving areas near the epicenter. Thousands of main line leaks were reported and repairs were time-consuming.

Among the numerous situations that contributed to the disruption of the water supply system was damage to Los Angeles Aqueduct No. 2 at Terminal Hill. Aqueduct No. 2 is made of 2.1-m (77 in) diameter steel pipes. Terminal Hill is located about 20 km (12.5 mi) north-northeast of the epicenter, southeast of the intersection of I5 and SR14. There is no strong motion record available for the site. However, two stations maintained by the California Division of Mines and Geology (CDMG) and the U.S. Geological Survey (USGS) about 5 km (3 mi) south of the site showed peak ground accelerations over 0.9g, indicating that the site probably was strongly shaken by the earthquake. Other indications of strong shaking can be seen from the numerous landslides along the mountainside to the north of the site (fig. 5.1), and the bridge failures at the intersection of I5 and SR14.

The reinforced concrete relief tank (surge chamber) on top of the hill appeared to perform well through the earthquake--no damage was observed (fig. 5.2). A steel pipe brings water up from the canyon below (fig. 5.3). The pipe is supported on concrete saddles built along the mountain slope. At a few places, the pipe separated from the saddles creating 50 to 80 mm (2 to 3 in) gaps. In at least one location, the pipe crashed vertically into the saddle. At two other locations, the pipe sections bulged 80 mm and 150 mm (3 and 6 in), however, no rupture or leakage was noticed. The ruptured section of the 2.1-m pipe is located near the hilltop. The two sections where the rupture occurred were connected using a mechanical coupling system (fig. 5.4). The pipe sections were connected by eight pairs of restrainer rods 35 mm (1-3/8 in) in diameter and 2.2 m (7 ft) long. The rods were attached to brackets, which were welded to the pipes. These welds broke during the earthquake (fig. 5.5) and resulted in the separation of the two pipe sections.

Repair of the pipe sections began immediately after the earthquake. The repair work was completed in the evening of January 19 and the aqueduct started operation at 2:00 a.m. on January 20. However, leakages occurred shortly thereafter, and the pipeline had to be shut down. Excavation was required to repair two other sections. The pipeline was back in operation on January 21.

The earthquake resulted in numerous breaks of water lines. Two water mains were ruptured at a site along Balboa Boulevard adjacent to the rupture of a 0.6-m (22 in) gas main. A major fire resulted, which is described later in this chapter.

There are two water reclamation plants in the Los Angeles area. The small one has a capacity of 75 000 m³/d (20 mgd) and the large one 300 000 m³/d (80 mgd). The larger facility, the Donald C. Tillman Water Reclamation Plant, is located in Van Nuys, southeast of the intersection of Woodley Avenue and Victory Boulevard. The inflow goes through primary, secondary, and tertiary treatment before the water is released for landscape irrigation and to a nearby lake for recreational use.

The earthquake resulted in damage to five out of twenty-two final clarifier tanks built in 1991 as part of the Phase II expansion. Twenty-two Phase I tanks built in 1983 were not damaged. Figure 5.6 shows a typical undamaged final clarifier tank. The scrapers are supported by railings attached to the walls with brackets. Chains are used to move the scrapers. All these components were made of plastic in the Phase II construction, whereas the brackets were made of metal and railings and sludge scrapers were made of redwood in the Phase I construction. Pins about 10 mm (3/8 in) in diameter and 19 mm (3/4 in) long connected the brackets to the railings. In the tanks where there was damage, it is suspected that the pins dislodged due to wave action in the tank and the railing became displaced. This caused jamming of the chain movement, which disabled the system (fig. 5.7).

Commercial power was lost at the Tillman plant during the earthquake. Interviews with plant personnel indicated that the emergency system, a 1500 kW diesel generator, was shut down by the operator when strange noises were heard. When the generator was restarted, sparks appeared and the emergency system was shut down again. As a result, the plant lost power for about eight hours. Fortunately, the plant did not lose its biological system, which is vital to restore normal plant operation. There was a low demand on the plant because the earthquake happened very early in the morning before daily activities normally begin to produce large quantities of wastewater.

Repair of the plant facilities was delayed due to nonstructural damage to the maintenance building. Warehouse stock which fell from shelves covered needed repair tools and equipment. It was two days before equipment could be moved out to repair the water treatment systems. The maintenance building offices suffered fallen ceiling tiles and air ducts. A few large glass panels in the reception area of the administration building were broken, but the building itself sustained no structural damage.

Figure 5.1.   Strong shaking at Aqueduct No. 2 at Terminal Hill can be inferred from the numerous landslides along the mountain slopes to the north of the site.

Figure 5.2.   The reinforced concrete surge tank at Terminal Hill performed well during the earthquake--no damage was observed.

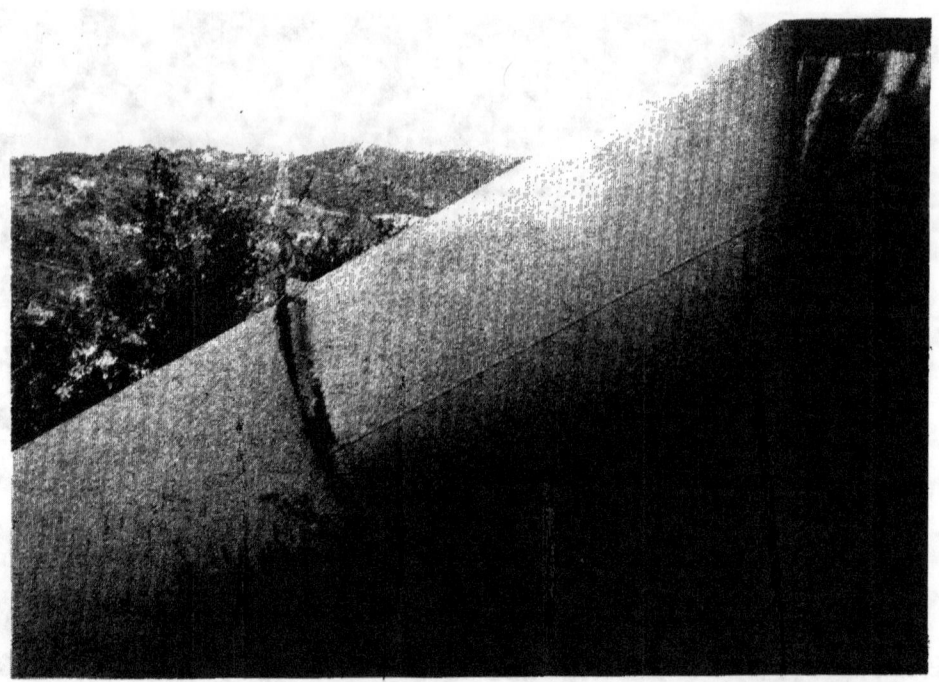

Figure 5.3.   The steel pipeline at Terminal Hill separated from its supporting saddle at several places and pipe sections bulged at other locations along the alignment.

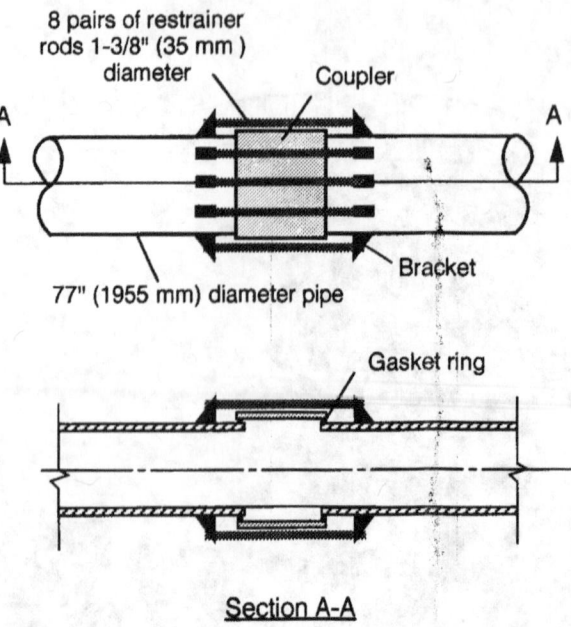

Figure 5.4.   Schematic drawing of connection of the two steel pipe sections which were pulled apart during the earthquake.

Figure 5.5.   Welds of the restrainer brackets broke as the result of strong shaking.

Figure 5.6.   Undamaged clarifier tank at the Tillman Water Reclamation Plant.

Figure 5.7.   A damaged sludge scraper in a clarifier tank at the Tillman Water Reclamation Plant.

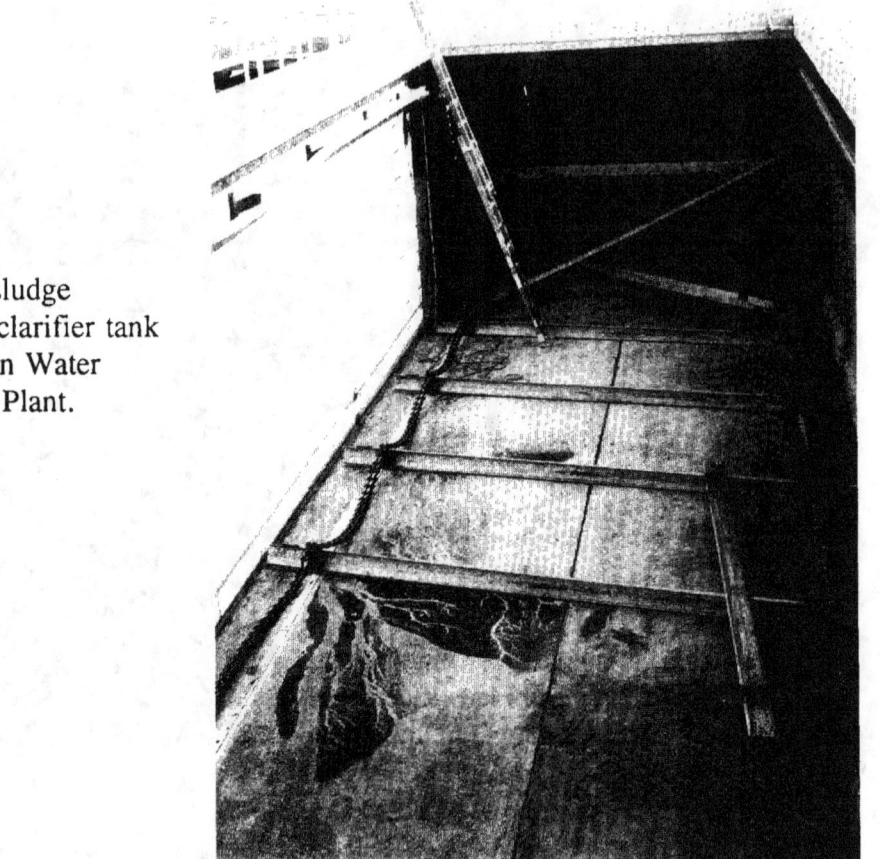

5.3 Gas and Liquid Fuels

Natural gas systems consist of transmission, distribution, and service lines. In the earthquake-affected area, transmission lines are steel pipes with diameters ranging from 0.3 to 0.8 m (12 to 30 in). Most of the failed lines were of pre-1971 construction. The distribution lines are either steel or plastic pipes. Compared with the 1971 San Fernando earthquake [15], this earthquake resulted in more ruptures in distribution lines than in transmission lines. Most breaks occurred to old steel pipes. Plastic pipes used in the distribution system seemed to perform well. About one hundred fires resulted from the rupture of gas lines. A number of fires were associated with the premature restoration of utilities, as discussed in chapter 6.

As in earlier earthquakes, such as the 1987 Whittier Narrows earthquake and the 1989 Loma Prieta earthquake, tens to hundreds of thousands of gas supply outages occurred. Most outages were due to customers shutting off gas valves for fear of gas explosions or fires. While the intent of this action is immediate safety, it can result in a long delay before service is restored because gas company technicians must test each system before turning the valve back on.

The rupture of a 0.6-m (22-in) gas main occurred along Balboa Boulevard between Rinaldi Street to the south and Lorillard Street to the north (fig. 5.8). Along this stretch, compressional ground failures occurred between Rinaldi Street and Halsey Street, and extensional ground failures occurred between Bircher Street and Halsey Street. Ground extension at this location is prominently exhibited by the transverse cracks in the pavement as shown in figure 5.9. Further, lateral spreading of 25 to 100 mm (1 to 4 in) toward the west was observed along the sidewalk on the west side of Balboa Boulevard north of Halsey Street, whereas no lateral spreading was observed on the east side of Balboa Boulevard.

Three pipelines ruptured as the result of ground contraction; a 150-mm (6-in) gas distribution line, the 1.8-m (68-in) Rinaldi trunk water line, and a 0.6-m (22-in) gas main (fig. 5.10). The Rinaldi trunk line was of post-1971 construction, and the gas main was of 1930 vintage. These pipes showed a shortening of 125 to 150 mm (5 to 6 in).

About one block north, the ground extension caused rupture of the same 0.6-m (22-in) gas main and a 1.2-m (48-in) water main (fig. 5.11). These pipes were pulled apart as the result of the ground extension. The rupture of the gas main caused a major fire at the site that destroyed five houses (figs. 5.12 and 5.13). The loss of both water mains at this location and the difficult access to the site due to the fire and street flooding made fire fighting difficult.

An excavated section just north of the fire site revealed some additional underground lines (fig. 5.14). The 460-mm (18-in) crude oil line in the middle of the photo performed well. The 150-mm (6-in) gas distribution line shown at the top of the photo is a replaced section.

In addition to the above damage in the epicentral area, the strong shaking from the earthquake cracked welds at several locations along a 250-mm (10-in) pipeline transporting crude oil from the San Joaquin Valley. As a result, there was an oil spill along the Santa Clara River.

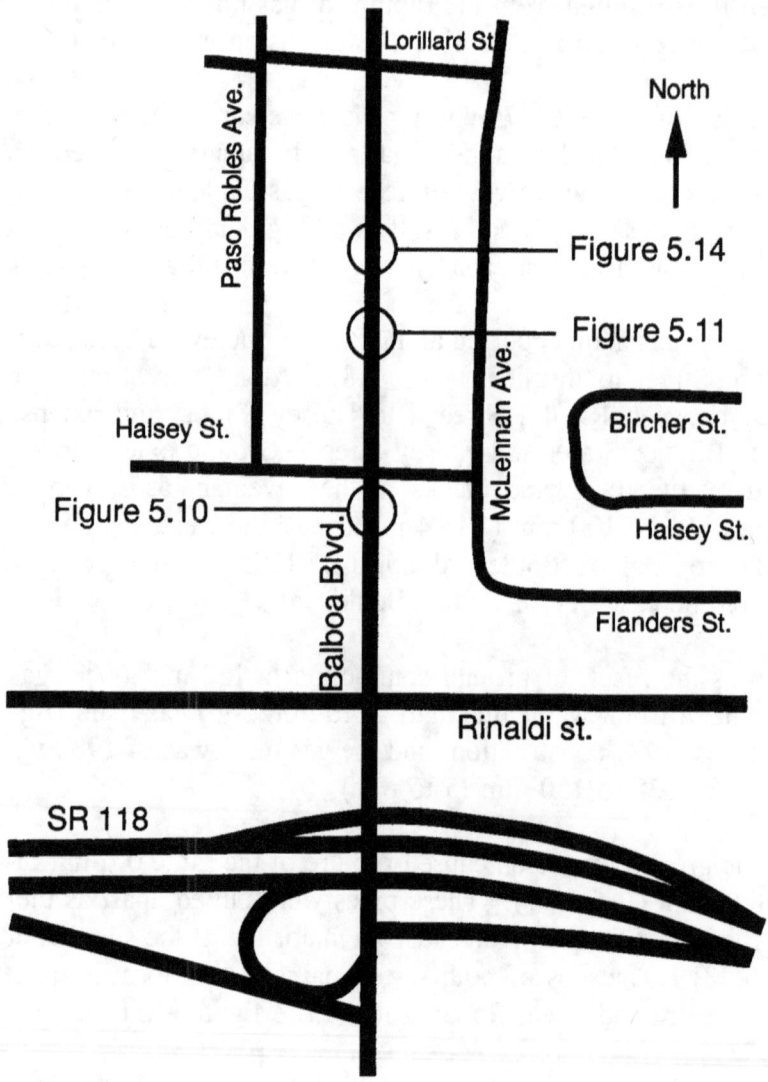

Figure 5.8. Location of the 0.6-m gas main rupture on Balboa Boulevard.

Figure 5.9.   Ground extension at the gas fire site on Balboa Boulevard can be seen by the transverse cracks in the pavement.

Figure 5.10. Ground contraction along Balboa Boulevard caused the rupture of a gas distribution line (top), the Rinaldi trunk 1.8-m (68 in) water main (center), and a gas main (bottom). The pipes were being repaired at the time this photograph was taken.

Figure 5.11. Ground extension along Balboa Boulevard resulted in the rupture of the same gas main shown in figure 5.10 (top) and a 1.2-m (48 in) water main (bottom). The rupture of the gas main here caused a major fire that engulfed five houses.

Figure 5.12. Houses destroyed by a fire resulting from the rupture of the 0.6-m gas main along Balboa Boulevard.

Figure 5.13. Houses destroyed by a fire resulting from the rupture of the 0.6-m gas main along Balboa Boulevard.

Figure 5.14. Some of the buried pipelines located near the intersection of Balboa Boulevard and Bircher Street showing the potential hazard of co-location of lifeline systems. At this site are three water lines (two of them main lines); three gas lines; two sewers; one crude oil line; overhead power, telephone, and cable TV lines; the street lighting system; and the street itself.

148

5.4 Electric Power

Power was lost to most of the Los Angeles basin area after the earthquake. Nearly 2 million customers were without service immediately after the quake. About half of them had power restored within one day and over 95 percent had power restored by midnight Tuesday, January 18. All power was restored within ten days after the earthquake.

Some transmission towers suffered significant damage, many as the result of foundation failure. Damage to several high voltage substations near the epicenter, such as Sylmar, Pardee, and Rinaldi, led to the widespread power outage in the Los Angeles basin, as well as isolated outages throughout seven western states (fig. 5.15). As happened during the 1971 San Fernando earthquake, porcelain elements of 230-kV and 500-kV equipment suffered the most damage (fig. 5.16). This highlights the urgent need for developing new earthquake-resistant materials to replace porcelain, which is very brittle. Furthermore, most of the 230-kV circuit switchers, similar to those at the Sylmar substation shown in figure 5.17, were damaged. However, none were damaged during the 1971 earthquake, a possible indication of much stronger ground shaking by the Northridge earthquake. Most of the capacitor banks, similar to those in the background in figure 5.17, performed well in this earthquake, whereas most collapsed during the 1971 quake. Better performance of the capacitor banks is the result of stricter seismic requirements in equipment qualification and in installation practices.

Figure 5.15. Damage to DC equipment at several high voltage substations, such as this one at Sylmar, led to widespread power outages in the Los Angeles area as well as isolated outages throughout seven western states. (Photo courtesy of Edward Matsuda, Pacific Gas and Electric Company.)

Figure 5.16. Porcelain is an integral part of high voltage electrical equipment due to insulation requirements and is also the most vulnerable to damage during strong earthquake shaking. (Photo courtesy of Edward Matsuda, Pacific Gas and Electric Company.)

Figure 5.17.   Most of the 230-kV circuit switchers (in the forefront) at the Sylmar substation were damaged. Most of the capacitor banks (in the background) performed well in this earthquake, whereas most collapsed during the 1971 quake. (Photo courtesy of Edward Matsuda of Pacific Gas and Electric Company.)

5.5 Transportation

All airports in the affected region survived the earthquake with no major problems. The airports were shut down immediately after the quake as a precautionary measure to allow inspection of runways and taxiways. All airports were re-opened for operation once the inspections had been completed. No structural damage was observed in airport facilities. However, they suffered some typical types of non-structural damage, such as fallen ceiling tiles and leakage of water pipes.

The earthquake caused a freight train derailment in Northridge (fig. 5.18). The 64-car freight train belonged to the Southern Pacific Railroad and was on its way from Houston to Sacramento. Twenty-five cars derailed, sixteen of which carried sulfuric acid or diesel fuel. The derailment resulted in the spill of 30 000 L (8000 gal) of sulfuric acid and 7500 L (2000 gal) of diesel fuel. There were no casualties in this incident. About 200 m (650 ft) of railroad tracks were replaced immediately following the earthquake and rail service was restored at 2:00 a.m., January 19. Removal of damaged cars and cleanup of debris were completed on January 21.

Strong ground shaking and lateral movement of subgrade materials resulted in numerous ruptures of asphalt pavement and concrete sidewalks in the epicentral area (figs. 5.19 and 5.20). In some instances, local traffic was interrupted temporarily until these cracks were repaired. In most cases, damage was minor and local traffic was not interrupted. The south approach of Balboa Boulevard at SR118 caved in because of loss of abutment fill due to a water main break (fig. 5.21). This bridge was closed for traffic due to some structural damage to the piers and the loss of the south abutment fill, as described in chapter 4.

Figure 5.18. Derailment of a 64-car freight train in Northridge. The incident resulted in the spill of 30 000 L of sulfuric acid and 7500 L of diesel fuel. (Photo courtesy of LeVal Lund.)

Figure 5.19. Transverse cracks in pavement along Balboa Boulevard in Northridge area.

Figure 5.20. Transverse cracks in pavement near the intersection of Balboa Boulevard and SR118.

Figure 5.21. The approach of Balboa Boulevard at SR118 caved in due to the loss of the abutment fill because of a water main break.

5.6 Summary

The Northridge earthquake offered an excellent opportunity to assess how the technology that has been used to shape the built environment performs when it is subjected to extraordinary natural forces such as those generated by a strong earthquake. A number of observations and some related conclusions can be drawn from the observations made immediately after the earthquake. Suggestions for improved practice are also provided.

5.6.1 Observations

- The earthquake resulted in much less damage to water treatment plant facilities than was caused by the 1971 San Fernando earthquake.

- The water supply system failed to provide service to customers because of widespread damage to the distribution system.

- Repair of water and gas lines is a very time-consuming process. Repairs should be thoroughly checked against leakage before backfilling pits.

- Repair of the Tillman Plant clarifiers was delayed due to nonstructural damage to the maintenance building that prevented operators for retrieving needed parts and tools. This delay could have been avoided if the building contents had been secured against earthquake motions.

- The earthquake resulted in relatively more ruptures in the natural gas distribution lines than in the transmission lines, when compared with the 1971 earthquake. Most of the breaks occurred in older steel pipes, whereas plastic pipes performed well.

- Power was lost to nearly 2 million people immediately after the earthquake. However, because of redundancy within the system, service was restored to over 95 percent of this population within 2 days.

- Some transmission towers suffered significant damage due to foundation failures.

- Damage to several high voltage substations near the epicenter contributed to the power outages in the epicentral area and to isolated outages throughout seven western states.

- Porcelain elements of 230-kV and 500-kV equipment showed high vulnerability to strong shaking, as they did in the 1971 earthquake.

- Lessons learned from the 1971 earthquake helped improve the performance of electric power systems, such as the capacitor banks, through stricter equipment qualification requirements and better installation practices.

- All airport facilities performed well. Some airport buildings suffered nonstructural damage.

- *The spill of sulfuric acid and diesel fuel caused by the railroad derailment in Northridge was*

155

brought under control within two days after the quake. Nevertheless, it demonstrated the potential hazard to an urban environment caused by spills of toxic materials.

5.6.2 Suggestions for Improving Practice

- There is a need to replace older gas lines built with brittle materials and connected with oxyacetylene-welded joints. Modern pipelines using ductile steel pipes and flexible joints performed well. Research is needed to develop cost effective methods to maintain the integrity of gas service lines during an earthquake to prevent the ignition of fires. Research is also needed to develop techniques to restore gas service to customers expeditiously without compromising fire safety.

- Reliability of the water supply after an earthquake is extremely important for fire fighting and for providing the water needed for other emergency purposes. Cost-effective techniques should be developed to replace older water mains. This is important because repair is extremely time-consuming and costly, especially for major pipelines. Improved techniques should also be developed to test the water-tightness of the repairs to avoid unnecessary delay in the restoration of service.

- Improved methods for avoiding damage to high voltage substations should be developed. New materials are needed to replace the brittle porcelain insulators. Better switch systems should be developed and installed to prevent blackouts. Failures of foundations for transmission towers should be thoroughly investigated.

- Disruptions of lifeline systems by an earthquake result in significant economic losses to society, even though loss of life may not be significant. Yet, lifelines have no nationally recognized seismic rehabilitation or design standards. Design criteria have been developed, updated, and used by individual utility companies. There is an urgent need for a national effort by the National Earthquake Hazards Reduction Program to develop nationally accepted design guidelines and standards for lifeline systems.

CHAPTER 6

POSTEARTHQUAKE FIRES

6.1 Introduction

The Northridge earthquake resulted in fires which challenged the resources of the fire service due to the number of fires, disruption of the water supply, and damage to fire protection systems within buildings. The majority of the estimated 30 to 50 significant fires were located in the San Fernando Valley and confined to the building of fire origin either by separation or by fire department action. Fortunately there was no loss of life from fire. A principal cause of the fires involved natural gas leaks. A small number of fires were caused by hazardous chemical interactions. The only major instances of building-to-building fire spread occurred in three manufactured housing developments (mobile home parks). Fire incidents occurred at a greater than normal rate in the days following the earthquake with the cause of some of the fires directly attributable to the restoration of power and gas to buildings shaken in the initial earthquake and aftershocks. Fire sprinkler systems sustained damage in some buildings although the number and extent of damage is not known at this time.

Fire protection in the municipal environment is derived from private and public systems including building construction, building fire protection systems, land use, public and private water supplies, public and private fire departments, and communication and utility systems. In the aftermath of a major earthquake the normal interactions between these systems are disrupted. Even though emergency operational plans exist, the interaction between these systems in reducing the loss from fire is complex since it involves decisions on the part of a great many people.

The loss of life and property caused by fire occurs in a different time frame than the structural and property damage caused directly by the earthquake. While most of the loss caused by by an earthquake occurs during the time of ground movement, there is basically no fire loss during that time. Fire loss directly attributable to the earthquake begins immediately following the ground shaking and can continue for days after the shaking has stopped.

This chapter examines the factors contributing to the cause, spread of and loss from fire in selected buildings affected by the earthquake. It is based on observations and interviews conducted primarily during the week following the earthquake, preliminary reports, and news media coverage and should not be considered comprehensive. The information presented is believed to be accurate although all of the facts could not be independently confirmed. A number of public and private agencies continue to compile and analyze more detailed information.

6.2 Fire Events Following the Earthquake

Immediately following the earthquake, the Los Angeles City Fire Department initiated the Earthquake Operational Mode which included placing emergency equipment on patrol throughout the city and dispatching fewer pieces of equipment to each incident in order to accommodate the increased number of incidents. Earthquake damage was widespread but occurred mostly within the City of Los Angles and most of the fire incidents were within the San Fernando Valley. Immediately following the earthquake, electrical power was lost and telephone service was disrupted throughout the city. At 5:45 a.m. Mayor Riordan declared a state of emergency. By 6:45 a.m. as many as 50 structure fires had been reported and over 100 incidents were being handled by the fire department. By 9:45 a.m. all fires were under control.

Although the epicenter was located within the City of Los Angeles, there was damage in surrounding counties and emergency resources throughout the region were utilized. In addition to responding to fire incidents, the fire department provided emergency medical, hazardous materials, and urban search and rescue services. The Los Angles City Fire Department responds to over 900 fire, medical, and other emergences on a typical day. This number increased to over 2200 on the day of the earthquake and remained at twice the normal level in the following days. The continued high number of incidents was due in part to fires associated with the restoration of utilities.

Water available for fire fighting was generally adequate in the San Fernando Valley area during the day following the Earthquake. The exceptions were in areas near the boundaries of the system and in areas at higher elevation. In the hours following the earthquake pressure in the water system dropped due to disruptions in supply and more than 3000 leaks. By the day after the earthquake, water tankers had been deployed throughout the San Fernando Valley to assist in fire fighting operations. On January 20th, fire department pumpers were used to pump water from areas with adequate pressure within the system to areas with low pressure.

6.3 Fire Causes

The 30 to 50 fires reported initially following the earthquake occurred in a variety of residential and commercial occupancies. Predictions of the number of fires following an earthquake have been made for some parts of the Los Angeles area, but not for the San Fernando Valley [25]. The majority of buildings in the San Fernando Valley are four stories or less in height and therefore the fires occurred primarily in these types of buildings. Figures 6.1 to 6.4 show some examples of buildings involved in postearthquake fires. The fire in the rear of the apartment complex shown in figure 6.4 was the only fire observed in a completely collapsed portion of a structure.

This chapter does not include a detailed investigation of the individual fires which occurred following the earthquake. Preliminary indications are that a significant number of fires were associated with natural gas leaks. Natural gas is the predominant fuel used for space and water heating in the Los Angeles area and can therefore be found in most buildings. Natural gas is not in itself a source of ignition, but is relatively easy to ignite in confined spaces. Although electrical power was lost throughout the area immediately after the earthquake, the most likely source of ignition was a combination of electrical sources and flames in the gas appliances themselves. Gas leaks occurred both inside and outside of buildings. As discussed in chapter 5, the fire resulting from a leak in a gas main under a street destroyed several nearby houses. Figure 6.5 shows a gas meter in a manufactured housing development (mobile home park) in which there were at least six individual ignitions. Although there was no leak in the gas service shown, it demonstrates how the movement of the manufactured homes during the earthquake damaged the gas service, resulting in leaks which were ignited by unknown sources. There were no postearthquake fires in the newest section of the development where an improved gas service design was used. As in past California earthquakes, water heaters appear to be a source of gas leaks [26]. Inadequately secured water heaters are likely to tip over during an earthquake. The fire which destroyed the multi-family housing unit shown in figure 6.6 was reported to have started as the result of damage to a water heater. An undamaged housing unit, similar to the one which was destroyed, can be seen in the background. Even though natural gas leaks may have played a role in a significant number of the 30 to 50 reported fires, this number is very small when compared with the total number of buildings exposed to significant shaking during the earthquake. Since residents of this area are aware of the dangers of gas leaks following an earthquake many fires may have been averted by individuals shutting off the gas to buildings or appliances.

The rapid failure of the electrical power distribution system probably resulted in fewer fires than might have been expected. As electrical and gas services were restored in the days following the earthquake, a significant number of fires were reported. Some of these fires were a result of earthquake damage to electrical and gas equipment which went unnoticed or unattended. Electrical and gas services were not disconnected in all red tagged buildings which were identified by authorities as unsafe to enter. These, and additional fires, may have all occurred immediately following the earthquake if electrical service had been maintained.

As in past California earthquakes, a small number of fires appear to have been caused by flammable liquid or chemical spills. Figure 6.7 shows a science building at the California State University at Northridge in which the fire was reported to have been the result of a chemical spill. No fires were known to have occurred at service stations. Since the earthquake occurred when most people were asleep, fire causes such as overturned candles and barbecue grills and fires associated with industrial processes appear to be nearly nonexistent.

A small number of wildland fires were attributed to earthquake related causes, most likely arcing in overhead power lines. Since the wind was light and the vegetation was not excessively dry, these fires were easily extinguished.

Figure 6.1. Fire damage in a single story commercial building.

Figure 6.2. Fire damage in a two story commercial building.

Figure 6.3. Fire damage in a three story commercial building.

Figure 6.4. Partially collapsed apartment building with fire damage in the rear.

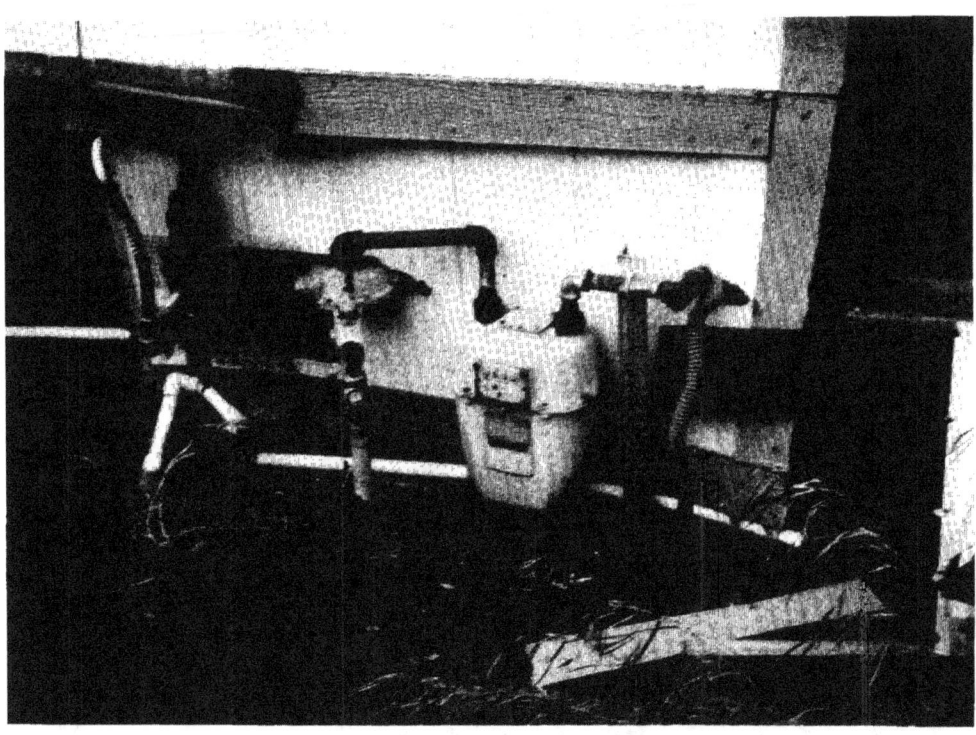

Figure 6.5. Damaged gas service in a manufactured housing development.

Figure 6.6. Multi-family residential building destroyed by fire.

Figure 6.7. University science building damaged by fire.

6.4 Fire Spread

Most building fires were confined to the building of fire origin due to a combination of factors including light winds, building construction, building separation, and the actions of the fire department. Experience and predictions of the impact of fire following earthquake indicate that at wind speeds above 9 m/s (20 mi/hr) the fire spread and associated loss will increase dramatically [25].

Building-to-building fire spread was limited to three manufactured housing developments (mobile home parks). Figure 6.8 shows the typical spacing between units in one of these developments. Figure 6.9 shows an area of the development destroyed by fire. Observations made at this development indicate that the method of unit-to-unit fire spread was primarily through windows. Once a unit became completely involved in fire, the thermal radiation was sufficient to cause the breakage of windows in an adjacent unit or to ignite combustibles within the unit directly through the windows. The fire department reported low water pressure in the area which combined with multiple independent fires and limited resources hindered fire fighting operations. The fire spread was stopped either by separation such as roads and open areas or by fire fighting operations.

A unique aspect of the construction of these manufactured units played a role in limiting fire spread and assisting fire department actions. As the units burned from the inside, the carport roofs collapsed from the building side, coming to rest on the outside supporting columns. In this way the carport roofs formed fire breaks as shown in figure 6.10. Although these roofs would not necessarily have survived the fire by themselves, they reduced the fire exposure on adjacent units and thus enhanced fire fighting operations.

Figure 6.8. Typical unit spacing in a manufactured housing development.

164

Figure 6.9. Impact of a multiple unit fire in a manufactured housing development.

Figure 6.10. Collapsed roof which acted as a fire break in a manufactured housing development.

6.5 Performance of Fire Protection Systems

Immediately following an earthquake, it is difficult to determine the performance of fire protection systems. Most of the systems can be inspected only from the inside of buildings, many of which are private, and the access to buildings is frequently restricted until structural safety can be determined. The most reliable source of data concerning these systems will come from repair and inspection records in the months to come.

Some damage to fire sprinkler systems has been reported but the full extent is not known. Damage to these systems is frequently the most visible of the fire protection systems since it may result in water leaks. Interviews with persons who entered buildings in the earthquake area indicate that many sprinkler systems remained intact, particularly those installed in accordance with latest seismic standards. Typical damage to fire sprinkler systems included broken pipes due to differential building movement or the sway generated in long pipe runs without adequate bracing. Sprinklers installed in the downward or pendent position from piping above ceilings were in some cases sheared off. In other cases, pendent sprinklers installed in drop ceilings were pulled through the ceiling by the upward movement of the pipes and punched new holes in the ceilings during the downward movement. While the punching may not have resulted in leaks, it damaged the sprinkler deflectors which generate the desired spray pattern. Damaged deflectors usually result in a significant decrease in sprinkler performance requiring the sprinklers to be replaced.

Sprinkler systems normally have one or more check valves to prevent water from flowing from the sprinkler system into the water supply system. In the most common wet pipe system, the sprinkler system piping will have the highest pressure attained in the water supply system over time. In the days following the earthquake, as the fire department pumped water from one part of the municipal water supply system to another, there were significant local increases in pressure. These higher pressures were then "trapped" in the sprinkler systems. Although it can easily be remedied by bleeding off the pressure, these higher pressures could lead to premature failure of the system and reduced effectiveness at the time of activation until the system returns to the design pressure.

Damage to fire alarm, detection, smoke control, other extinguishing systems, and passive building fire protection systems such as fire and smoke barriers has not been reported at this time. The disruption of land based communication systems is reported to have affected the ability of systems to dispatch alarms.

6.6 Summary

The Northridge earthquake provided the opportunity to examine the strengths and weaknesses of the infrastructure designed to deal with postearthquake fires. Examining fire events associated with each major earthquake provides a means to reinforce continually the successes and provide insight into possible improvements.

The following items contributed to the low loss of life and property due to fire following the Northridge earthquake.

- The time of day during which the earthquake occurred reduced traffic and hazardous operations

  The earthquake occurred before the start of morning traffic on a federal holiday and most people were at home and traffic was light. This resulted in few traffic accidents which would have required fire department resources, and minimized traffic would have impeded the flow of emergency vehicles. Since most business and industries were not operating at the time of the earthquake, the fires and injuries associated with these types of activities were minimal. Most people were at home and relatively few were trapped in collapsed structures. Trapped victims require significant emergency resources to locate and rescue, and some of these resources are the same as those used for fire fighting.

- Light winds lead to reduced fire intensity and spread

  On the day of the earthquake, the winds were light and, based on news media video coverage, played almost no role in increasing fire intensity within buildings or promoting building-to-building fire spread. This was a most fortunate circumstance since high winds would have certainly lead to a far more serious fire situation. There is no practical method available to protect large numbers of closely spaced buildings from building-to-building fire spread, particularly during high wind conditions.

- Adequate moisture content in wildlands reduced the fire hazard of natural fuels

  The wildland fires reported immediately following the earthquake were quickly extinguished. If the wildland moisture content and relative humidity had been low and the winds had been high, major wildland fires could have followed the earthquake. The devastation caused by wildland fires has been experienced many times in the past in the Los Angeles area.

- Fire department plan for responding to postearthquake emergencies

  Following an earthquake, the fire department has primary responsibility for responding to a wide variety of emergencies, and the ability to manage the emergencies effectively can substantially reduce the loss of life and property. The Los Angeles City Fire Department has a comprehensive plan for dealing with postearthquake emergencies which is reevaluated following each major earthquake. The state of California has a sophisticated system to provide mutual-aid from neighboring communities during major emergencies which was utilized during the Northridge earthquake.

- Improvements in seismic building and fire standards

An analysis of code compliance and recent seismic related changes is beyond the scope of this investigation. There is some evidence however, that in the area of fire sprinkler systems for example, systems installed in accordance with the latest seismic standards withstood the earthquake with little damage. Since most of the fire safety systems are not visible from the outside of buildings a complete analysis of these systems can be made only when repair and inspection records become available.

The following have been identified as areas for possible improvement in reducing the loss of postearthquake fires.

- Protection of natural gas service lines and appliances

Although the absolute numbers are relatively small, damage to natural gas pipelines and appliances resulting in leaks contributed to a significant fraction of the postearthquake fires. This would indicate that a further study of the impact of earthquakes on building gas service and appliances is warranted.

- Plan to restore utilities after the earthquake

Fires directly attributable to earthquake damage continued to occur in the days following the earthquake. Most of these fires were caused by the restoration of power to buildings damaged in the earthquake. Some of these were red tagged buildings which had been identified by authorities as unsafe to enter. Others were buildings which were either unoccupied or in which hazards had not been identified. This issue places at odds the desire to restore utility service as quickly as possible and the desire not to cause additional fires. There are no nationally recognized standards or recommended practices which address this issue. The state-of-the-art computer-assisted dispatching system being installed by the Los Angles City Fire Department may offer a means of maintaining building status and perhaps, via sensors, utility system status and even seismic activity [27].

- Improve means of communicating emergencies to authorities

This is perhaps one of the most challenging opportunities for reducing the loss of life and property following an earthquake. Following the Northridge earthquake there was significant disruption to telephone and other land based communication systems. Although government agencies such as fire, law enforcement, and utilities maintained contact with field units via radio, many citizens were unable to report requests for aid via telephone. The present method of locating emergencies by placing public service personnel on patrol and utilizing helicopters, while most likely the best method presently available, is still inadequate. This is an area where emerging communications technologies may provide significant improvements. It should be noted that even if there had been no damage to communications systems, processing the vast quantities of information needed to make critical decisions is a significant challenge in itself.

- Predictions of postearthquake fire losses

  Models which predict the number of postearthquake fires and the spread of those fires can be useful tools for developing earthquake response plans. Predictions have not been developed for an earthquake centered in the Northridge area. At this time it cannot be determined if the available models would have accurately predicted the fire loss experienced in the San Fernando Valley or the loss which would have occurred with higher winds. The fire loss data which will become available for the Northridge earthquake can be used to verify the predictions of the fire loss models.

Fortunately the Northridge earthquake occurred when winds and traffic were light, most people were at home, and the humidity was relatively high. If the earthquake had occurred when there were Santa Ana winds, a high volume of traffic, and low humidity, the loss of life and property from fire most certainly would have been far greater.

CHAPTER 7

CONCLUSIONS AND RECOMMENDATIONS

7.1 Conclusions

The initial assessment of the Northridge earthquake of January 17, 1994, provides significant lessons for public policies and construction practices in earthquake prone areas throughout the United States. While it was not in a category of large earthquakes in terms of its magnitude, the Northridge earthquake caused severe damage to a wide range of structural types because the epicenter was located in a populated urban area. Damaged structures revealed a number of deficiencies in current construction practices and areas needing improvements in code provisions. Implementing lessons learned about structural performance and postearthquake fires will reduce seismic hazards throughout the United States.

7.1.1 General

1. The Northridge earthquake claimed 58 lives and caused over 1500 serious injuries. However, fewer than half of the deaths were attributed directly to structural failures. Because it occurred at 4:31 a.m., on a holiday, life loss was limited to a small number. Had the earthquake occurred during business hours, the collapse of parking structures alone could have caused a large number of deaths.

2. Although a number of fires started immediately following the earthquake, calm winds limited spreading of fires in residential and commercial districts. At mobile home parks, fires spread from unit to unit. In most instances, fires were caused by natural gas leaks.

3. Damage to multi-family dwellings contributed significantly to the over 25 000 dwelling units that became unhabitable. Providing adequate shelter for displaced persons is a major task after an earthquake. Special attention should be paid to improving the seismic performance of existing dwelling stock.

4. At many locations, peak ground acceleration exceeded 0.4g, the maximum design value in building codes. However, most buildings met code expectations for performance. Because many strong motion records and response measurements are available from this earthquake, valuable opportunities exist for in-depth studies of building performance to assess the adequacy of design values for earthquake forces and provisions for seismic resistance.

7.1.2 Building Performance

1. In many cases, buildings designed and constructed in accordance with modern (mid-1970's or later) seismic requirements performed well structurally. This clearly shows the value of incorporating modern seismic design and construction requirements into building codes. However, failures of structures characterized as "Undefined Structural Systems" (Uniform Building Code Section 2333(i)2), such as the parking garage at California State University

at Northridge, indicate that the performance of such structural systems needs to be evaluated carefully to update code provisions.

2. Damage to unreinforced masonry (URM) buildings was widespread. In most cases, those URM buildings rehabilitated with parapet braces and floor-wall ties, such as those rehabilitated in response to the Los Angeles Division 88 ordinance, escaped total collapse. However, walls sustained severe cracking and, in many cases, pieces fell onto sidewalks. This posed life-threatening hazards to pedestrians.

3. Nonstructural damage caused hospitals, schools, businesses, and industrial facilities to be inoperative even though structural damage was minimal or non-existent. An in-depth review of current code requirements and standards for nonstructural elements is needed to improve their seismic performance.

4. Damage to steel structures was not readily visible from the exterior of buildings because most steel members are hidden behind architectural finishes and fire proofing. Removal of such coverings revealed brittle failures of welds and connections in many steel frame structures. Because owners of damaged structures often wish to keep damage reports confidential, damage information is not forthcoming. Detailed failure analyses of available data should be performed to understand the underlying causes of these failures.

7.1.3 Bridge Performance

1. In general, bridges designed using standards developed after the mid-1970's performed well. Several bridges near the epicentral region, which were designed and constructed in the 1960's and early 1970's, sustained severe damage. Of the seven major bridges which sustained severe damage, six failed due to inadequate lateral reinforcement of the bridge piers.

2. Most older bridges which had been seismically retrofitted (with cable restrainers, pier jacketing or foundation strengthening) performed well in the Northridge earthquake. However, because this earthquake was relatively moderate in magnitude, it should not necessarily be concluded that all seismic retrofit methods for bridges have been adequately proof tested by this event. Design criteria for cable restrainers may need to be reviewed. Even though jacketed bridge piers apparently performed well in this earthquake, it would be valuable to study the intensity of ground motions experienced at the specific bridge sites where jacketed piers have been employed, so that the performance of jacketed piers in larger events can be estimated.

3. It is likely that some bridge piers were damaged because their effective lengths had been reduced. Several factors reduced the effective lengths: architectural flares at the tops of piers; backfill soil over a portion of the pier height; and concrete walls cast integrally with, or directly abutting, piers. Such constraints need to be minimized, or the effects of the constraints must be considered carefully in the design of piers.

172

4. In bridges with piers of varying heights, the shortest piers tended to sustain the most damage. This is apparently because short piers have high lateral stiffnesses, and therefore attract a large share of the seismic loads. A better understanding of the role of short piers in overall bridge performance, is needed.

5. Bridge spans which had skewed alignments or irregular plan configurations often sustained severe damage. Special attention should be paid to the potential for problems with bridges having skewed alignments or irregular plans.

6. Older bridge bearings, of the steel rocker type, are highly susceptible to damage during strong ground shaking. Loss of rocker bearing support can lead to a broad range of bridge damage, including cracked girders, loss of roadway elevation alignment, and complete collapse of the superstructure.

7.1.4 Performance of Lifelines

1. Damage to older trunk lines and main lines for water distribution caused serious disruptions in water supply in the epicentral region. About 50 000 Los Angeles Department of Water and Power customers were without water on the first day after the earthquake. About 10 000 customers were still without water one week after the earthquake.

2. Buried pipelines which carry natural gas and oil fractured at many locations due to ground motion. Over 1300 breaks and leaks in the gas piping system were reported.

3. As in past earthquakes, brittle ceramic elements, which are often the weak links in circuit breaker assemblies, were damaged.

7.1.5 Fire

1. The occurrence of the earthquake before the start of morning traffic on a federal holiday allowed the fire department to respond to fires promptly without delays.

2. Damage to natural gas pipelines and appliances resulting in leaks contributed significantly to postearthquake fires.

3. In many cases, electric power was restored to buildings which were identified as unsafe for entry. The desire to restore utility service as quickly as possible is at odds with the desire not to cause fires.

4. In general, fire sprinkler systems designed and installed in accordance with the latest seismic standards withstood the earthquake with little damage. However, in some instances, sprinkler pipes ruptured where sprinkler systems interacted with suspended ceilings.

7.2 Recommendations

7.2.1 Performance of All Structures

1. **A comprehensive assessment of the performance of structures in relation to ground motions of the Northridge earthquake should be made.**

Preliminary spectral analyses of free-field strong motions revealed that many structures may have been subjected to a seismic demand greater than that prescribed by the current code. This earthquake provides a valuable opportunity to evaluate successful and unsuccessful performance of structures designed according to the modern seismic design requirements. The reliability of currently used vulnerability assessment methodologies can also be assessed.

2. **The effects of vertical accelerations on the performance of structures need to be investigated.**

Unusually high vertical accelerations were recorded at several locations in the epicentral region. Studies of the influence of such high accelerations on structural performance are needed to determine whether high vertical accelerations were a contributing cause of structural failures. The adequacy of current design provisions for effects of vertical accelerations should be evaluated.

7.2.2 Building Performance

1. **Develop design and construction criteria that provide protection against property loss and maintain postearthquake functionality.**

Current building codes are intended to protect life safety. Thus, adherence to the seismic requirements of building codes is not sufficient to prevent damage. The Northridge earthquake again demonstrated this limitation of modern building codes. Reliable tools should be developed to allow designers and constructors to serve owners who desire buildings that can remain functional after a design-level earthquake with a limited level of damage.

2. **Educate building designers, constructors and regulators to recognize and produce earthquake resistant structural systems.**

Buildings having stiffness and geometric irregularities performed poorly during this earthquake. No building code can anticipate every possible building design and be written to prevent all potential undesirable performance. It is possible for every element of a building to meet code requirements, yet for the building as a whole perform poorly in an earthquake. Insightful use of the code by the designers, constructors and regulators is needed to obtain the desired performance. Education is needed to transfer the knowledge on building performance gained from this and other earthquakes to the people who can apply these lessons on a daily basis.

174

3. **Code requirements for the deformation compatibility of structural members need to be re-examined.**

The lateral displacement capacity of structural members which are designed to carry primarily vertical loads may not be compatible with that of lateral load resisting structural members. Due to this incompatibility, failures of vertical load carrying members may occur. This may precipitate total or partial collapse of a structure.

4. **Comprehensive studies of the performance of unreinforced masonry buildings, both rehabilitated and unrehabilitated, should be carried out to evaluate the effectiveness of rehabilitation methods.**

Although parapet braces and floor-wall ties apparently prevented total collapse of unreinforced masonry buildings during the earthquake, large pieces of walls fell, creating life-safety hazards. More effective measures are needed to reduce life-threatening hazards.

5. **In-depth evaluation of current code requirements and standards is needed for interactions between and attachments of nonstructural elements.**

Structurally sound buildings sustained major damage to nonstructural elements such as suspended ceilings and light fixtures. These failures can be a life safety issue. Attachment of nonstructural elements and displacement compatibility of nonstructural systems with structural elements and with each other should be examined.

6. **Ductility and energy absorption capacity of welded connections and joints of steel frame structures need to be investigated to improve design and construction requirements in codes and standards.**

Many failures of weldments, welded connections and joints have been reported since the initial field investigations of the earthquake affected area. Damage was found at beam-to-column connections of a building located at as far as 32 km from the epicenter. Brittle failures of welded connections should be documented and evaluated carefully to assess the reliability of this type of connection under seismic loading.

7. **Performance of buildings that had been rehabilitated prior to the Northridge earthquake should be studied to confirm the validity of, or to improve, standards for strengthening existing buildings.**

A variety of data on performance of rehabilitated buildings are available from the Northridge earthquake. A significant opportunity is available to evaluate and improve practices for the strengthening existing buildings, including rehabilitation methods for systems known to be vulnerable, such as unreinforced masonry and non-ductile concrete frames.

7.2.3 Bridge Performance

1. Cost-effective seismic retrofit guidelines should be developed for multiple-pier bridge bents.

To date, most seismic retrofit studies have been directed towards strengthening isolated piers. Comparatively little has been done to address the strengthening of multiple-pier bents.

2. Specifications and guidelines should be developed for the design and retrofit of bridge spans with skewed alignments or irregular plan configurations.

Skewed overcrossings on I5 at Gavin Canyon and on SR118 at Mission-Gothic sustained severe damage. Studies should be carried out with two objectives: to understand the fundamental response of skewed bridges to seismic loads; and to develop methods for mitigating damage in existing and planned skewed bridges.

3. The seismic performance of short bridge piers and the role which short piers play in the overall seismic response of bridges should be studied.

A number of short bridge piers were severely damage in the Northridge earthquake. Some of these piers were under-reinforced, but others contained amounts of reinforcement close to those that would be specified using current design codes. The implications of these failures for the design of future bridges should be studied. In addition, the effective lengths of some piers were reduced by constraints such as adjacent concrete walls, backfill soil and architectural column flares. The effects of such constraints on column behavior need to be investigated.

4. The seismic performance of rocker type bridge bearings should be evaluated and retrofitting techniques should be developed.

Rocker type bearings failed during the Northridge earthquake. Similar types of bearings are used throughout the Central and Eastern United States, where there is significant potential for seismic activity. Studies should be carried out to develop methods for rehabilitating or replacing steel rocker bearings.

7.2.4 Performance of Lifelines

1. Analytical, laboratory, and field studies of the performance of electrical distribution systems, and of gas and water pipelines should be conducted to develop improved vulnerability assessment and retrofit practices.

There were extensive failures occurred at electric switch yards and in buried pipelines in the epicentral region. Similar failure potentials exist in all seismically hazardous areas of the United States.

2. **Develop cost effective methods to maintain the integrity of gas service lines during an earthquake to prevent the ignition of fires.**

There is a need to replace older gas lines built with brittle materials.

3. **Develop methods for rehabilitating old steel water pipelines.**

Older steel water pipes sustained damage during the earthquake, resulting in interruption of the water supply to homes and businesses. More importantly, the loss of water lines jeopardized fire fighting capabilities. Methods for rehabilitating water pipes without replacing them are needed. Such methods can be used throughout the earthquake prone regions of the United States.

4. **Nationally applicable design and construction provisions for new and existing lifelines should be developed.**

The Northridge earthquake revealed again the importance of successful lifeline performance for the prevention of life, property and other losses due to earthquakes. In contrast to buildings, no nationally applicable design and construction practices are available for new and existing lifelines.

7.2.5 Fire Safety

1. **Develop criteria to reduce the postearthquake fire hazards posed by gas service lines and appliances.**

A significant portion of the earthquake-induced fires were caused by damage to gas service lines or to gas appliances. These failures should be studied so that improved criteria for postearthquake fire safety of gas service lines and appliances can be developed.

2. **Develop criteria and techniques to allow utility personnel to assess the safety of restoring electricity to damaged buildings.**

Building fires continued to ignite in the days following the earthquake. Most of these fires were caused by the restoration of power to buildings damaged in the earthquake.

3. **Develop postearthquake fire models to aid emergency planning.**

Fire hazard prediction methodologies should be developed so that emergency managers can better plan pre-event prevention actions and post-event responses. Data from the Northridge event and other recent earthquakes should be used to verify the efficacy of the model.

CHAPTER 8

REFERENCES

[1] Porcella, R.L., Etheredge, E.C., Maley, R.P., and Acosta, A.V., *Accelerograms Recorded at USGS National Strong-Motion Network Stations During the M_s=6.6 Northridge, California Earthquake of January 17, 1994*, U.S. Geological Survey Open File Report 94-141, 1994.

[2] Hall J.F., editor, *Northridge Earthquake January 17, 1994, Preliminary Reconnaissance Report*, Earthquake Engineering Research Institute, 94-01, Oakland, CA, 1994.

[3] Dunbar, P.K., Lockridge, P.A., and Whiteside, L.S., *Catalog of Significant Earthquakes 2150 B.C. - 1991 A. D.*, National Geophysical Data Center, National Oceanic and Atmospheric Administration, National Environmental Satellite, Data and Information Service, Boulder, CO, 1992.

[4] Hauksson, E., Jones, L., Mori, J., Heaton, T., and Hutton, K., *Aftershocks of the Magnitude 6.6 Northridge, California Earthquake of January 17, 1994*, Southern California Seismographic Network, California Institute of Technology, Pasadena, CA, 1994.

[5] Moehle, J.P., editor, *Preliminary Report on the Seismological and Engineering Aspects of the January 17, 1994 Northridge Earthquake*, Earthquake Engineering Research Center Report No. UCB/EERC-94/01, University of California, Berkeley, CA.

[6] International Conference of Building Officials, Int., *Uniform Building Code*, Whittier, CA, 1991.

[7] Lew, H.S., editor, *Performance of Structures During the Loma Prieta Earthquake of October 17, 1989*, National Institute of Standards and Technology, NIST Special Publication 778, Gaithersburg, MD, 1990.

[8] *Rapid Visual Screening of Buildings for Potential Seismic Hazards: A Handbook*, FEMA 154, Federal Emergency Management Agency, Washington, DC, 1988.

[9] Building Officials and Code Administrators International, Inc., *The BOCA National Building Code*, Country Club Hills, IL, 1989.

[10] Structural Engineers Association of California, *Recommended Lateral Force Requirements and Commentary*, Sacramento, CA, 1990.

[11] Applied Technology Council, *Procedures for Postearthquake Safety Evaluation of Buildings*, ATC 20, Redwood City, CA, 1989.

[12] Los Angeles County Coroner, *Northridge Earthquake Cases 2-14-94*, 1994.

[13] City of Los Angeles, *Building Code - City of Los Angeles 1990 Amendments*, Los Angeles, CA 1990.

[14] Deppe, K., "The Whittier Narrows Earthquake of October 1, 1987 - Evaluation of Strengthened and Unstrengthened Unreinforced Masonry in Los Angeles City," *Earthquake Spectra*, Volume 4, No. 1, pp. 157-180.

[15] Lew, H.S., Leyendecker, E.V., and Dikkers, R.D., *Engineering Aspects of the 1971 San Fernando Earthquake*, Building Science Series 40, National Bureau of Standards, Gaithersburg, MD, 1971.

[16] Jenning, P.C., editor, *Engineering Features of the San Fernando Earthquake, February 9, 1971*, Earthquake Engineering Research Laboratory EERL 71-02, California Institute of Technology, Pasadena, CA, 1971.

[17] Willman, David, et.al, "Shaky Bridges, Shaken Theories," *The Los Angeles Times*, February 16, 1994, pp. S2-S3.

[18] Federal Highway Administration, "Seismic Retrofitting Guidelines for Highway Bridges," Report FHWA/RD-83/007, 1983.

[19] Federal Highway Administration, "Seismic Retrofitting Manual for Highway Bridges," prepared by the National Center for Earthquake Engineering Research, State University of NY at Buffalo, FHWA Contract DTFH61-92-C-00106, November, 1993 (draft).

[20] State of California, Dept. of Transportation (Caltrans), Office of Structure Design, *Memo to Designers*, Section 20, "Seismic", Sacramento, CA, 1989, with revisions to 1994.

[21] State of California, Dept. of Transportation (Caltrans), "Seismic Safety Retrofit Program - Annual Report," February 1, 1994.

[22] Priestley, M.J.N., Seible, F., and Uang, C.M., *The Northridge Earthquake of January 17, 1994, Damage Analysis of Selected Freeway Bridges*, Report SSRP-94/06, Dept. of Applied Mechanics and Engineering Sciences, University of California at La Jolla, CA, Feb., 1994.

[23] State of California, *The San Fernando Earthquake: Field Investigation of Bridge Damage*, Business and Transportation Agency, Dept. of Public Works, Division of Highways, Bridge Dept., 1971.

[24] "The January 17, 1994 Northridge Earthquake, Bridges, Slide Set," produced by the Earthquake Engineering Research Center, University of California at Berkeley, March 1994.

[13] City of Los Angeles, *Building Code - City of Los Angeles 1990 Amendments*, Los Angeles, CA 1990.

[14] Deppe, K., "The Whittier Narrows Earthquake of October 1, 1987 - Evaluation of Strengthened and Unstrengthened Unreinforced Masonry in Los Angeles City," *Earthquake Spectra*, Volume 4, No. 1, pp. 157-180.

[15] Lew, H.S., Leyendecker, E.V., and Dikkers, R.D., *Engineering Aspects of the 1971 San Fernando Earthquake*, Building Science Series 40, National Bureau of Standards, Gaithersburg, MD, 1971.

[16] Jenning, P.C., editor, *Engineering Features of the San Fernando Earthquake, February 9, 1971*, Earthquake Engineering Research Laboratory EERL 71-02, California Institute of Technology, Pasadena, CA, 1971.

[17] Willman, David, et.al, "Shaky Bridges, Shaken Theories," *The Los Angeles Times*, February 16, 1994, pp. S2-S3.

[18] Federal Highway Administration, "Seismic Retrofitting Guidelines for Highway Bridges," Report FHWA/RD-83/007, 1983.

[19] Federal Highway Administration, "Seismic Retrofitting Manual for Highway Bridges," prepared by the National Center for Earthquake Engineering Research, State University of NY at Buffalo, FHWA Contract DTFH61-92-C-00106, November, 1993 (draft).

[20] State of California, Dept. of Transportation (Caltrans), Office of Structure Design, *Memo to Designers*, Section 20, "Seismic", Sacramento, CA, 1989, with revisions to 1994.

[21] State of California, Dept. of Transportation (Caltrans), "Seismic Safety Retrofit Program - Annual Report," February 1, 1994.

[22] Priestley, M.J.N., Seible, F., and Uang, C.M., *The Northridge Earthquake of January 17, 1994, Damage Analysis of Selected Freeway Bridges*, Report SSRP-94/06, Dept. of Applied Mechanics and Engineering Sciences, University of California at La Jolla, CA, Feb., 1994.

[23] State of California, *The San Fernando Earthquake: Field Investigation of Bridge Damage*, Business and Transportation Agency, Dept. of Public Works, Division of Highways, Bridge Dept., 1971.

[24] "The January 17, 1994 Northridge Earthquake, Bridges, Slide Set," produced by the Earthquake Engineering Research Center, University of California at Berkeley, March 1994.